THE EXTINCTION OF
THE PRICE TAG

To Rachel—

with much

love

THE EXTINCTION OF THE PRICE TAG

HOW DYNAMIC PRICING CAN SAVE YOU

SAHAJ SHARDA

NEW DEGREE PRESS

THE EXTINCTION OF THE PRICE TAG
How Dynamic Pricing Can Save You

ISBN   978-1-64137-080-6   *Paperback*
ISBN   978-1-64137-081-3   *Ebook*

To Mom, your sacrifices haven't gone unnoticed.
You've made my success possible.

To Dad, I've learned everything from your example.

To Nanaji and Naniji and Bauji and Bai, your
unrelenting love and support is my north star.

CONTENTS

INTRODUCTION 1

THE CONTEXT

1. THE GOOD OLD DAYS.. 19
2. TECHNOLOGICAL SHIFTS 29
3. CULTURAL SHIFTS... 45
4. WHAT IS A PRICE REALLY? 59
5. A BASIC ECONOMIC FRAMEWORK OF PRICES.................... 71
6. HOW PRICES ARE PERCEIVED.............................. 81

DYNAMIC PRICING MODELS

7. WHEN IS DYNAMIC PRICING BEST? 95
8. FIXED RULES DYNAMIC PRICING.. 107
9. REVENUE MANAGEMENT DYNAMIC PRICING 121
10. CONDITIONAL RULES DYNAMIC PRICING 135
11. PERSONALIZED PRICING 147

CONSUMING SMARTER

12. HOW DO CONSUMERS BENEFIT?.. 165
    CONCLUSION.. 173
    BIBLIOGRAPHY 183

INTRODUCTION

———

Imagine the scene.

You're sitting in a plush red chair at the cinema. In the center of the third row from the very back, you're relaxing quite comfortably after a long, exhausting week. Your friends are sitting on either side of you, sharing snacks. As your friends pass the popcorn from side to side, they whisper comments to one another, and the movie plays in the background. When the popcorn is finally passed to you, you notice that you're very quickly getting to the bottom of the bag. Suddenly, there's a loud thundering noise from the speakers. Fearfully, you jump in your seat. You look around. Your entire row is shocked, all your friends are sitting up. In the film, the protagonist has been shot by the villain. What will happen to the hero? Your heart beats quickly because you know that the fate of the world hangs in the balance…

The screen goes blank. It's intermission. Still coping with the suspense of whether or not the protagonist is going to die, you and your friends decide to find refuge in munchies and drinks. As you line up for concessions, you look up at the prices and find that the prices have increased substantially from when you first came into the movie theater. A medium popcorn and a small soda are now twenty dollars when that same combo used to be twelve dollars less than an hour and a half ago. *What a rip-off…*

Still, you're starving and thirsty; moreover, you can't leave the theater now, because intermission is about to end, so what can you do? You grumble something about price gouging to the concessions attendant, and hesitantly you fork over the premium for a medium popcorn and small soda.

After your purchases, you sit back down in your seat. The movie continues, still seriously wounded from the gunshot wound, the leading man is rushed to the hospital in the back of an ambulance. As the supporting cast wear looks of horror and determination on-screen, the doctors at the hospital do all they can. Soon, the patient is hooked up to an electrocardiogram, a machine that plots the electrical activity of the heart. We all watch in shock and suspense, as the machine plots a line that spikes and falls with each beat of the heart. Then, the unthinkable happens. The robust spikes and dips are replaced with a flatline. The patient, our hero, is dying.

The doctors bring out a defibrillator, the electrical paddles that the doctor rubs together and then slams on the patient's chest in an attempt to electrically shock his heart into working. Almost always, the doctor succeeds, and we all breathe a collective sigh of relief. Without fail, the camera pans to the electrocardiogram, where the graph has resumed its periodic spike and dip pattern. Life goes on.

It's this gripping visual image that can perhaps best represent the difference between static and dynamic pricing. The flatline graphically represents a price staying constant, a fixed or static price. In dynamic pricing, the price changes over time, spiking and dipping periodically. In fact, the prices you and your friends paid for your popcorn and soda were dynamically fluctuating. Those prices spiked and dipped just like a living patients heart rate.

Just as, in the movies, where doctors inevitably use technology to reanimate the flatline, today, a handful of CEOs and business leaders are attempting to use technology to reanimate the price line. Uber, Lyft, Amazon, and many other tech firms have their hand on the defibrillator, and they are starting to rub the paddles together, as the American economy and, increasingly, the global economy lay on the operating bed.

While a movie's plot can represent dynamic pricing symbolically, increasingly the very act of going to the movies can represent it literally:

- Depending on, among other factors, the showing time, any given movie's popularity, and the number of tickets still available, theaters are now changing their prices constantly to try and maximize revenue.
- Buying a pair of seats 20 hours before a showing is suddenly very different from buying those same seats 20 minutes before that showing. You probably already know this from your own experience.
- Have you bought tickets on Ticketmaster? Have you used the Atom Tickets app to buy tickets?
- Are you planning on going to Regal Cinemas anytime soon? Dynamic pricing is increasingly capturing commerce in cinema, and cinema is far from the only industry to feel the coming shifts.

Who is behind this change? What exactly is changing? When did this start? Why is it happening? Where do we go from here? Naturally, as with any economic shift, there are many questions and, initially, few answers.

The most general definition of dynamic pricing is any pricing strategy where the price is not fixed to a certain amount but rather can change from person to person, time to time, and transaction to transaction. Most likely, you've interacted with dynamic pricing in some limited way in the past. It might have even benefitted you.

One Friday night last January I went out with all my good friends to a happening nightclub in Washington DC. It was freezing that night, so we all bundled up in layers of sweaters and jackets before we hopped in a cab to get there. Yet, as soon as we walked into the nightclub, we started to feel the distinctly different temperature. One of my close friends looked at me and said, "Wow, it's really hot in here." We took off our jackets immediately, but the club didn't have a coat check. I told my friend, "I'm just going to leave my jacket near the bar, we'll get them on the way out." That was a big mistake.

We went on to have a fantastic night, but suddenly around 2 AM, the club started closing. Herded out by the bouncer, my friends and I forgot our jackets, the ones we had carefully placed near the bar, as we headed outside. As soon as we got outside, we started shivering uncontrollably. We tried going back in but the quite formidable bouncer told us, "You can't go in, the club is closed." His tone made it quite clear that there wasn't a debate to be had. Truly miserable in the cold, we decided to cut our losses and get a cab, but none were available.

There were roughly a hundred people outside of this club all trying to get a cab in the freezing cold. My friend pulled out his phone, biting the bullet, and called an Uber with a massive surge multiplier. Within minutes, our Uber was there, and we were extracted from the bitter wilderness to go home to our closely controlled climates back at the Georgetown dorms.

That experiment served as a sort of natural experiment for me to understand the power of dynamic pricing. Cabs don't dynamically price, and correspondingly there was little incentive for cab drivers to come to a club at 2 AM on a freezing night. Because of this, there was a substantial deficit of cabs when we needed one. Alternatively, Uber does surge pricing and there is a significant enough incentive for Uber drivers to come to that same club at the same time in the same temperature. Clearly, something was working with dynamic pricing.

Many of us have probably had similar experiences with Uber or Lyft, in fact that is a key component for why those companies are so successful. Yet, that dynamic pricing is happening at all, really goes against the grain of how commerce has been conducted for most of the last two centuries. In fact, since the industrial revolution, the conventional wisdom has almost always opposed any attempt to introduce dynamic pricing. Historically, dynamic pricing has been perceived as wrong, alienating, and arbitrary. Just ask Douglas Ivester, the former CEO of Coca-Cola.

While under Ivester's leadership as CEO in 1999, Coca-Cola executives realized they could stick a thermometer on vending machines and adjust prices according to the weather. They surmised that the weather could serve as a proxy measurement for demand, since more people want a nice chilled Coke when it's hot out than when it's cold. Coca-Cola thought it could increase profits and lower waiting times when it was hot, and according to Ivester, "It is fair that [Coke] should be more expensive" at these times (Leonhardt). After he made that comment, however, the media fallout was catastrophic. This heresy would not be tolerated in the court of public opinion.

To clarify, at this stage Coca-Cola had not implemented the idea. Coca-Cola had simply floated the idea of potentially testing this dynamic pricing technology in some vending machines. Mr. Ivester's comment and Coca-Cola's plan was the corporate equivalent of dipping one's toe in the water. Yet, the backlash was shocking. People were upset, they were angry. They had never witnessed or conceptualized dynamic prices within this context before. They thought Coca-Cola would price gouge them especially when they wanted the Coke most. One particular executive, in the beverage industry, grumbled, "What's next? A machine that X-rays people's pockets to find out how much change they have and raises the price accordingly?" (Hays). Moreover, Coca-Cola's competitors attacked them in public. In fact, Pepsi stoked the fire, trying to exploit the negative sentiment. Pepsi spokesman John Brown said, "we believe that machines that raise prices in hot weather exploit consumers who live in warm climates," and he then followed up his statement with other criticisms of Coca-Cola and praise for Pepsi (Hays).

The mob won out. Instead of trying to explain their rationale, Coca-Cola backed out. In their view, the backlash was too overwhelming. So, they didn't stick to their decision. They abandoned their intuitive understanding of the economics of vending machine purchases. Instead, they buckled under public pressure before even trying the idea. Moreover, Mr. Ivester, the CEO who was ostracized in the press, walked back his statement in favor of dynamic pricing.

Going back decades, this has been how almost every new dynamic pricing initiative has been received. The script almost never changes. Some innovative business will try to push for dynamic pricing to increase its own profits, and consumers will uproar until the business retreats. Following the same corporate-consumer dance, the conventional wisdom has crystallized around the idea that dynamic pricing is unwise for companies.

Yet, that crystallized conventional wisdom is beginning to crack. Companies like Uber and Lyft, Amazon and eBay, Priceline and even the Golden State Warriors are throwing out that jaded script. Instead, they are charting a bold new path to vitalize or revitalize their respective businesses. And why not? Just take a look at the numbers:

As the MIT Sloan Management Review concluded in 2007 about dynamic pricing in retail, dynamic pricing "can improve revenues and profits by up to 8% and 25%, respectively." (Sahay). Think about that. That range is just the theoretical potential of this pricing strategy in one industry.

Empirically, at Ford Motor Company, billions of dollars of additional profits have materialized over the last two decades. This story of success is the same as American Airlines, Marriott International, FedEx, UPS, and on, and on. Billions of dollars of profit have been generated for companies bold enough to delve into dynamic pricing and deft enough to manage public opinion.

To date, the gains have mostly been limited to certain industries, such as transportation and hospitality. Now imagine, if we could achieve that kind of gain across all industries. It is not a stretch to say that dynamic pricing could revitalize the entirety of the American economy. While this proliferation has begun, there is still a lot left to do, and in too many cases, the conventional wisdom reflexively opposing dynamic pricing remains unchanged.

When I was twelve years old, I asked my dad what the stock market was. He showed me his portfolio, he showed me some charts for some of his stocks, he explained how stock prices went up and down. I found the graphs to be elegant. Tracing my finger along the computer screen, I could trace the fluctuation in demand for any given stock. Then, I asked my dad, "Why don't all prices move like this?" He responded, "Because only the stock market works like that." His answer was empty, and the moment was fleeting, it would be years before I considered the notion of dynamic pricing again.

Last summer, my college roommate, Aaron, and I were trying to come up with an idea for a startup. I was always told that lightning never strikes the same spot twice, but for some reason it did. Over the summer, as I lay in bed, a variation of that same idea, from when I was twelve, popped up in my head in a moment of inspiration. It was a fleeting thought, randomly traveling through my consciousness. I don't know how, but suddenly I was considering why restaurant prices did not move up and down like stock prices did? After all, demand for food goes up and down throughout the day, just like demand for a stock throughout the day. Within weeks of having that initial thought, I launched Dynos, a company dedicated to helping restaurants dynamically price. Since then, Aaron and I have built an entire platform dedicated to helping businesses dynamically price so that we can do our part to invigorate the American economy.

The truth is dynamic pricing is a relatively easy concept to understand, but as I've learned—and you'll learn as well from discussions with some of the world's leading thinkers and innovators on pricing—there are a lot of factors involved in implementing it successfully.

A lot.

That's why I've written this book, to unpack the concept for a much broader audience of innovators, executives and entrepreneurs who have contemplated implementing dynamic pricing and to diffuse what I've learned so that others can do the same thing. Dynamic pricing affects two sides of the market. Producers and consumers. This book is therefore also for both of those sides. While most lessons can be broadly applied, the lessons in this book have a special focus on producers and consumers in *perishable* goods markets like dining, transportation, and sports.

If you're a business, particularly in perishable goods markets, you'll learn:

- from noted professors of economics why it is inevitable that dynamic pricing takes hold in your market;
- all the different dynamic pricing strategies that you can employ, illustrated by a thought experiment on the streets of Morocco;

- from the former-CEO of Savored about how marketplaces are allowing restaurants to fill up during empty hours using fixed rules dynamic pricing;
- from Dynos, the former CTO of Priceline, and numerous small business owners about how you can use dynamic pricing to your advantage without tripping on consumer backlash; and
- you'll learn from a Nobel Laureate in economics about how big the impact of dynamic pricing can be.

In other words, you'll learn step by step about how you can use a tool that has the potential to increase your profits substantially.

On the flip side, if you're a consumer, in perishable goods markets:

- you'll learn from people designing dynamic pricing algorithms about how dynamic pricing can benefit you, as well as
- you'll learn tricks to maximize your own benefit from fluctuating demand and its impact on dynamic pricing. For example, Uber drivers will teach you how to avoid surge pricing, while Roger Sterling from Mad Men will teach you how to not fall victim to cognitive biases.

For both sides of the market, this book will also consider the ethics of dynamic pricing. When does dynamic pricing cross the line into shady and manipulative? Does it do so when the cost of an Uber surges after a snowstorm? Is charging different people, different prices, at the same time, ethically appropriate? What does "dynamic" mean in a philosophical sense anyway?

I've spent the last year, researching, developing, and deploying every insight I convey to you. I've spoken to experts in every field. I've considered and criticized what they've had to say. I've applied what they've taught me. I've done so first for my startup and then for this book. It is with great consideration that any content in this book has been written.

Yet, my motive is something larger than just profit. For whatever reason, dynamic pricing feels personal to me. I've never been good with "good enough". I'm a child of the Great Recession. I grew up watching people lose their jobs and their homes. Maybe that's why I've become fixated on *optimizing* our economic systems. You see, it's not about winners and losers in the world of dynamic pricing. Dynamic pricing isn't a way to maximize profits for the business at the cost of the consumer. It's actually about optimizing the pricing and profit for *everyone* in the transaction. Take for example Uber, who has been an innovator in the world of dynamic pricing in the transportation industry. Some decry Uber's practices as exploitive when they add 2x, 3x, or even 10x increases in base fares due to "surge pricing." But the flip side is, this leads to an increase in the supply of drivers who can give rides. In the case of New Year's Eve when you might *never* be able to get a taxi and if you do they might decide they don't want to take you where you want to go, surge pricing gets more drivers out and enables you to find a ride even if it's more expensive. The alternative might be driving yourself or frankly just being stuck. And the Uber experiment has certainly had benefits, with numerous studies linking a drop in drunk driving accidents and arrests to the service operating in that city, including finding a 25 to 35 percent decline in New York City alcohol-related accidents since Uber was launched there (Irby). Or, as in my case, the benefit can be saving you from being stranded outside a nightclub in freezing weather.

And while there are examples of successes like Uber—despite the periodic consumer frustrations surge pricing creates—the problem is, through fixed prices, we've been doing nearly all pricing in an inefficient way. Before there were technological constraints that required fixed prices. Today, only the perception problem is holding back mass adoption, and innovators in every field are finally realizing that. Great opportunity lies ahead for those who can maneuver the dangerous waters of dynamic pricing optics. After all, from a theoretical economic perspective, the consensus is clear. Fixed prices are bad for producers and they are bad for consumers. They decrease economic activity and they create waste.

Just consider this story. Imagine that a college student waits in the line for the vending machine for five minutes. It's 90° outside. The AC isn't working inside. He is sweating while he stands in line, waiting. By the time it's finally his turn, he is already incredibly frustrated. He takes out his cash, and in his impatience, he drops it. He grumbles angrily as he picks it up again. He inserts the crumpled dollar bill in quickly, he clicks on the Coke button and the button doesn't do anything. Other than the sound of his repeated clicking of the button, there is a startling silence. In the absence of the hum of the machine retrieving a Coke, frustration really boils up. He is supposed to have a bottle that is refreshingly cold right now. The college student presses the button again and again and again. Still nothing. He bangs the vending machine as hard as he can. As his hand stings, he stares down at the analog in anger, the vending machine says sold out.

Transport yourself to Mr. Ivester's shoes as the CEO of Coca-Cola in 1999. In light of that story of that college kid, does it make sense to say that increasing prices during high demand can sometimes leave consumers better off because higher prices ration a product and decrease wait times? If you were the CEO of Coca-Cola, would you have walked back your comments in 1999, or would you have tried to change the stagnant status quo?

The main idea you'll discover in this book is simple: despite what the conventional wisdom says, the coming wave of dynamic pricing is inevitable. This is because consumer perceptions are changing, through a sort of "pricing contact theory", and because technological shifts are making dynamic pricing too lucrative. Before it used to cost too much to change price tags and reprint menus; because everything is now electronic, today it costs far too much not to.

If used judiciously, dynamic pricing can be a force for good.

After all, it already has been.

PART 1

THE CONTEXT

CHAPTER 1

THE GOOD OLD DAYS

———

Our species, Homo Sapiens, evolved roughly 200, 000 years ago. Yet, for almost the entirety of our time on this planet, our population never made it past 5 million people. Then, 12, 000 years ago, the first farmer planted his or her seeds. Today, the human population is 7.6 billion people and growing.

Someone give that guy a raise.

Anthropologists and economists have always wondered how exactly the modern economy came to be. We know that trade grew massively after the start of the agricultural revolution 12, 000 years ago. Beyond that, there are various theories, about which economic structures prevailed in our early days. Some argue that there were command economies, where some centralized authority doled out goods. Others argue that there were gift economies, where people would trade in favors, without immediately asking for anything in return. Think of this as an economy full of IOUs. Alternatively, Adam Smith, the father of economics, believed that humans first conducted trade through barter in their movement towards development. The truth is, no one really knows. Not yet anyway.

All we know is throughout our history, negotiations have always played a central role in facilitating the exchange of goods. There's an old joke that illustrates this well. Two men, a farmer and a peasant, go to a trade and barter market. The farmer is a middle-class man who needs to sell all his produce in order to run his household, so he negotiates toughly with all his customers and makes only the shrewdest deals. The peasant is a man of simple tastes; he's just looking to trade honest labor for a good meal. But he has been ripped off by others at the market before and wants to make sure he's getting a square deal. At the market, the peasant runs into the farmer. He asks, "Mr. farmer, can I have an apple in exchange for an honest day's work?" The farmer, being a shrewd fellow, hands him an apple with a worm in it, the one no one else wants to buy. Quite hungry, the peasant takes a big bite of the apple. He chews for a bit, his jaw movements slowing as he tastes the worm. Finally, he swallows with a sour look on his face and looks down at the apple. Angrily, he looks back at the farmer and says, "Mr. farmer, you've conned me!" Pointing at the apple, he continues, "This apple only has half a worm in it!"

As the peasant can indicate, wanting the best deal, even when we might not know what that is, is embedded within human nature. Whether its an auction house in antiquity, a bazaar in the present, an alehouse in 17th century England, or a street cart in 12th century China, since the invention of agriculture, the exchange of goods has almost always been determined by people negotiating back and forth, haggling over the price. In fact, in many places around the world, it still is that way today. At least that's what my Uncle Ajay tells me.

Ajay grew up in India in the 1980s and 1990s. He grew up in a commercial city, with workers hustling through the streets throughout the day. There were some sections of town, where entire streets were consumed by informal markets, of street carts and caravans, and during the weekdays the entire street would fill with thousands of people, all trying to get the best deals for household goods. Against this backdrop, Ajay's family, ran a metal cutlery stand in one of the busiest streets in town. It was a tough business. Day after day of negotiating allowed even the average person on the street to become an expert at reading people. Sellers would cry about how they were being robbed, as they made deals to make buyers feel better. Buyers would make a whole show of being on the verge of starving to get better deals from sellers. As Shakespeare once said, "All the world's a stage," and nowhere is that truer than Gwalior, India.

One day, Ajay's grandfather who usually ran the stand went home for an afternoon tea break. In elementary school, Ajay pleaded with his grandfather to be allowed to guard the stand while his grandfather went home. He was a kid. There was no real reason for him to stay at the stand. In an attempted robbery, he could do absolutely nothing to protect the merchandise. The truth was that Ajay just loved watching all the people pass by on the street. His grandfather really didn't want to leave him alone but decided that he didn't want to deal with Ajay nagging him all the way home and back. So he left Ajay at the stand, but he made it clear that he was allowed to be there only under one condition: He told Ajay point blank, "If anyone tries to buy anything while I'm gone, tell them the store is closed until I return." That message went in one ear and out the other.

Ajay was alone, in charge of the family metal cutlery stand, for less than one hour; however, the stand was located on the busiest street of the main market in Gwalior. So person after person, would stop by the store and ask Ajay what prices were for certain goods. Ajay, wanting to be able to stay at the store alone in the future, heeded his grandfather's advice. He kept telling everyone that came to the store, "sorry we're closed!" Yet, the store had a kiosk-y format whereby potential customers could see all the inventory of stand. So person after person, would point at something and offer a pile of cash to Ajay for a good, and all that money was starting to tempt him.

Still, he persevered and waived people away. Until he physically lost all patience, Ajay was sitting there on the stand, when a customer arrived and said to him, "Hey you, I'll give you this pile of cash for four brass plates." In Ajay's mind, what he needed to do was clear. His grandfather had given him strict instructions not to engage. But in his heart, he couldn't resist. he was going to run this store one day anyway, might as well get some practice, he thought. The precocious shopkeeper that he was, Ajay replied back, "No, I'll only sell them at ten rupees a plate!" The customer laughed. He removed a few bills from the pile he was offering Ajay, and said: "You drive a hard bargain!" What had happened was that Ajay had quoted a price even lower than what the customer was willing to pay per unit. Ajay felt very stupid, but he'd already made the offer, what could he do at this point?

Ajay dug around in the back for the brass plates in an attempt to stall. He looked at the horizon hoping his grandfather would walk in. The customer, rather impatiently, pointed out where the inventory he wanted was. Ajay had no clue what to do, but the sale had already gone too far for Ajay to back away now. Social expectations weighing on his shoulders, Ajay handed the guy the four brass plates that he was pointing at. The deal was done.

The issue was that what Ajay had foolishly considered a reasonable price for the plates, turned out to be the best deal this potential customer had ever heard of in his life. Before Ajay knew it, the customer disappeared into the crowd, probably holding the brass plates like trophies from a hunt. When his grandfather returned, Ajay knew he would have to do something. He said to his grandfather desperately, "while you were gone, someone came and stole four brass plates, I couldn't do anything to stop him." HIs grandfather, surprised, asked a series of questions: "what did he look like?" "Where did he go?" "did you know him?" Ajay short on details, just said, "I don't know." Worried, his grandfather asked the other shopkeepers, but no one else had seen the theft. Eventually, his grandfather settled down. The next day dozens of people came to the family metal cutlery store in search of brass plates at ten rupees a plate. His grandfather put two and two together and Ajay was grounded for months.

While Ajay's fate was tragic, the real point of that story was to illustrate how negotiation-based many developing economies are throughout the world. Prices are not fixed in any tangible way, and if they are not fixed they are by definition dynamic, changing from transaction to transaction. When framed in that way, it becomes quite clear that dynamic pricing is nothing new, it used to be the most common way to transact throughout history. In fact, it is a historical anomaly that prices are largely fixed here in the developed world. It didn't use to be that way. In fact, static or fixed prices were the exception, not the rule until the industrial revolution in the United States. To quote the song *Cotton Eye Joe*, you may be wondering about fixed prices, "where did you come from, where did you go?"

Maybe nothing in life so satisfying as ripping off the tag on the beautiful new shirt that you just bought. The sound as the plastic snaps is cathartic. How many times have you ripped off the tag? Hundreds of times? Thousands? Every time the joy is almost infinite, if momentary.

Further, there is nothing more ubiquitous as the symbol of capitalism than the price tag. Yet, today that symbol is dying and changing, and in the metamorphosis, new things are emerging. But where did the price tag come from in the first place? And just how recent are our price tags? And what about the idea they represent- static or fixed pricing?

The price tag is a fairly recent phenomenon, and it is a phenomenon that ushered in fixed prices. Before price tags, everything was a negotiation. Store clerks, who knew the individuals in their community, would drive a hard bargain. Customers came into the shop ready to pay as little as they possibly could, and store clerks were trained in order to extract as much money from each buyer that they possibly could. For example, if I wanted to buy a loaf of bread, I'd tell the clerk I was checking out a loaf of sourdough. The Clerk, knowing that I was driving around in a new car, would charge me something more than I usually paid. No, I'd say, that price is too high! As the metaphorical music played in the background, there was this same dance every time you had to buy something.

In fact, the price tag didn't really exist until it was invented by two department stores, Wanamaker's in Philadelphia and Macy's in New York, both of which standardized the concept of static prices in the late 19th century (Goldstein, Phillips, and Jiang). Maybe the invention of a little slip of paper that you attach to goods was a freak accident. Maybe it was totally random that these two men, John Wanamaker and Rowland H. Macy both pioneered the concept. Yet, there were two underlying reasons that bound the destiny of these two men together:

Firstly, cultural norms. Quakers, in particular, were opposed to bargaining historically. As a people committed to a religious tradition that deeply promoted equality, Quakers found it unjust that different people would pay different prices. It's no accident then, that John Wanamaker, a man from Philadelphia, a location embedded with Quaker ideals, and Rowland H. Macy, a Quaker himself, would promote the invention of price tags, a written guarantee of the same price for everyone. In fact, John Wanamaker, a deeply principled man, committed himself to the idea that since we are all the same before God, we ought to pay the same prices.

Secondly, economic reasons. The negotiating dance I outlined before was time-consuming and it was expensive to train store clerks to know all the information about each individual good in the store. The overarching idea behind department stores is that there is a large volume of transactions every day. A prerequisite for that is fast transactions. So, these department stores wrote a price down on little slips of paper and they stuck it on their merchandise. There is an economic cost that they paid for that, they were losing out on revenue from people who would have possibly paid more, and they were losing out on revenue from people who would've paid less, but because the price tag set a price that was too high for them, they were no longer willing to purchase the good. Yet, it was Macy's estimation that those costs were outweighed by the benefits of faster and cheaper transactions. It's an economic decision and that idea of fixed prices proliferated. It proliferated to other department stores. It proliferated to smaller stores. It proliferated to catalogs.

When the late 19th century companies like Sears started to build catalogs, the concept of fixed prices got a big boost (Thompson). Serving as a proto-Amazon, Sears would collect orders by mail and ship items by rail all over the continental United States (Thompson). A catalog is a pamphlet, not a person. You can't negotiate with the catalog. So customers became acclimated to seeing a fixed price listed on a piece of paper. Slowly through department stores and catalogs, this idea became embedded in the American psyche. Frankly, less negotiating was just more convenient.

In the history of economic transactions, I think that if there's one directionality it is towards minimizing, not only the time but importantly the friction that is involved in getting a trade done. It's hard to get people to admit that they want something. It's hard to get them to exchange. When you can decrease all those external variables that are affecting people from pulling the trigger, then you increase the speed, quantity of transactions and increase the satisfaction people get from them.

Given the primitive technology of the time, Macy's changed how we conduct transactions, and largely we still conduct transactions through fixed prices because of that innovation. However, that process that they invented, it's getting changed again. This time, too, we're seeing something fully new emerge. We're seeing something even faster, better primed for this information age, ready to change the way we transact. We're watching the extinction of the price tag.

CHAPTER 2

TECHNOLOGICAL SHIFTS

———

One day, my mom got a phone call. The man on the phone said, "Ma'am, there's a delivery man here for you. He's asking where should he leave the TV." My mom replied back, "I never ordered a TV." The man said, "Ma'am, he says he has the receipt with him. Can I send him to your apartment?" As it turns out, she really *didn't* order a TV.

But a cheeky three-year-old lad had figured out this newfangled thing called "buying online" through the internet browser on our family's computer.

See, I was savvy even at three.

In those days, we had a massive desktop computer in our apartment, and the computer came with a dial-up internet connection. I don't remember those days well, but supposedly, that meant that the computer would make a series of annoying phone sounds every time someone tried to open a website. It also meant that all connections were super slow. It would take more than a whole minute to load a website in its entirety.

One day while my mom was opening up her email, she decided to leave toddler-me near the computer, while she went to check on something in the other room. She thought she would be back before the website was done loading. While she was gone, an ad had popped up on the computer, and I had somehow fumbled onto the keys and pressed a sequence of random buttons. When my Mom got back, all she saw was a pop-up that said thanks for your order. Odd.

It wasn't until the TV showed up at our door that she realized what I had done. I guess I've always had expensive tastes. My dad spent the next week on the phone with the TV company, trying to return the TV. Eventually, a delivery man came to our door, and just as the TV came into our lives, so too did it go away. With that, my first encounter with e-commerce ended in failure.

Nearly two decades ago, when that story took place, e-commerce was just getting started. It was not even close to being a primary way for people to conduct transactions. In fact, computers themselves were rare. The internet was just starting to reach a critical mass of people. That story aside, for most of my early childhood, I wasn't even allowed to use a computer.

When I was seven years old, my friends at school started playing games on the internet. Every day, they would come to school and report on their new high scores. One day, my friend asked me, "Have you played the new Star Wars game?" I hadn't, and every day it was becoming more and more obvious that I was clearly missing out on something massive.

In those days, my family only had one laptop in the house at the time, probably because we didn't really need it all that much. My parents mostly used it for email, and other work-related stuff that I didn't understand. However, it was a peripheral tool, at best. The laptop was in the office room upstairs, and I had been told by my dad, that I was forbidden from touching it. He had all of his work files stored on that computer.

The slick operator that I was, whenever my dad was out running errands or taking a nap, I would sneak up the stairs. The trick was to tip-toe when you were going up the stairs, and as long as the stairs didn't creak, my mom would never notice that I was going upstairs. Once I made it to the top floor, I was golden. The laptop didn't even have a password. It's like they wanted me to play games on it.

One day my dad caught me. My dad walked into the office, and he saw me sitting in his chair, his laptop open. He was livid. He roared, "What are you doing in here?!?" Emotional and feeling guilty, I started crying. I showed him the game I was playing. He looked me in the eyes and he said, "If you ever need to use the computer, you need to ask me." He paused, before he continued, "Go to bed."

I couldn't sleep that night. In the middle of the night, I got out of bed to find him. The office door was open. As I walked in, I saw flashing lights on the laptop screen. He was playing the Star Wars game that I had been playing earlier when he caught me. Little by little, computer technology and the internet started to become more pervasive. People, like all my friends, started using the internet for gaming. Soon people like my dad caught on. Others started using the internet more and more for communication.

As the computer and the internet gained universal acceptance, another technology exploded onto the scene to accelerate this trend. On January 9th, 2007, Steve Jobs took the stage and introduced the iPhone to the world. The Smartphone and its cousin the tablet has since proliferated all over the world. this is one of the primary drivers of the dynamic pricing revolution going on in the status quo because now. As Scott Case, the founding CTO of Priceline explains, "you've got ubiquity in smartphones, the amount of customers who have access to the tools."

When my niece was 4 years old, she watching *Dora the Explorer* on the Youtube app on her iPad. When you see a toddler being able to maneuver that technology, you realize that literally anyone now has the ability to manipulate smartphones and tablets. More importantly, these are devices, primed with critical computing power, small enough to fit in our pockets. You never have to be without a portal to the cyber-world again.

At the same time, companies like Amazon and eBay started to spring up. These sorts of companies are called marketplaces. They serve as exchanges where buys and sellers can connect with each other and conduct transactions. Slowly, the ubiquity of the internet gave way to commerce increasingly being done online. In 2016, Amazon alone did roughly $46.6 Billion worth of e-commerce sales.

These tectonic technological shifts have transformed how commerce is conducted. The proliferation of marketplaces and direct-to-consumer sites have also paved the way for the abolition of fixed pricing, because of a few very simple reasons:

Firstly, these websites slash menu costs. Menu costs is a term that economists created to refer to the cost of changing prices. For example, when a restaurant changes its prices it has to print more menus, and that costs something. Now changing a price online costs nothing, you simply need to type in the new price on a keyboard. This term also represents other costs. For example, it costs something to inform customers that prices have gone up or down, through advertising. Websites spread information for you, cost-effectively. Customers can find what they are looking for in a marketplace, and the price changes are obvious to them. Because it now costs next to nothing to change prices, changing prices as a strategy is proliferating in the market.

Secondly, access to information has gone up. Before a person only really knew what things cost in and around his or her area. Now, through eBay, we can find people willing to sell what we want 3, 000 miles away. This spread of information makes people incredibly well informed. Because of this, dynamic pricing strategies have more efficacy. For example, one strategy is to peg your prices to that of a competitor, with a slightly lower margin. Because savvy consumers will have access to information about prices across the market, this is a way to capture significant market share from a competitor. Moreover, this is uniquely possible because of technological shifts. In the past, people either wouldn't know that someone else could sell for cheaper, or companies wouldn't be able to track the prices of their competitors. Now all the information you need is available online.

The problem now is that there is too much information available. In fact, prices are just another piece of information adding to that information overload. Now if you add to all that information, the fact that prices are always changing, how is a consumer supposed to square all of that and make a decision, there's too much to think about!

It is clear that for e-commerce, and dynamic pricing, to work there needs to be some structure. This is so that information, such as price changes, is delivered in a timely efficient way that people can understand. Consequently, dynamic pricing, particularly in informal markets, is intimately connected to marketplaces. It is not enough to simply change your prices on your own website because a lot of times customers are not going to check every individual store's website. However, if all of the stores are aggregated in one place, now all of a sudden it is very simple for customers to compare prices, especially if they are changing. Thus, arise marketplaces. These are apps and websites that organize particular markets so that you don't get lost in a black hole of information overload. One good example of an early marketplace is Zaarly.

Zaarly has now become a home services marketplace, where people looking for home cleaners or plumbers can be matched with people who provide those services and are guaranteed to provide a service of sufficient quality. However, it started off as a marketplace for people looking to hire others to perform any task. In fact, the story of Zaarly follows a simi-lar arc to that of e-commerce more broadly. E-commerce was initially disorganized. On websites like Zaarly, anyone could get anything.

As Eric Jorgenson, a marketplace expert and one of the initial members of the team at Zaarly explained about the service, "We were demand focused and so we saw like all these random new use cases come up like we were delivering groceries before Instacart. We were giving rides before Uber and Lyft. People were renting cars before Getaround." However, the directionality over time has been for these marketplaces to formalize around specific applications and website services. As Eric continued he explained that, "We saw all these use cases so early, that has now been picked off by like huge marketplace companies that have verticalized and built amazing tools around specific things."

Zaarly itself doesn't interfere with the pricing decisions of its vendors; in other words, it doesn't actively usher dynamic pricing, but other marketplaces that have grown out of similar concepts in many cases do. Think about eBay for example, the price that the same item is sold at in two different eBay auctions can vary.

Today, part of the reason dynamic pricing works well for ride-sharing like Uber is that people go to one place, and the company does everything for them, giving them the price in a neat format. As the internet becomes faster, as phones reach ever greater audiences, as more information becomes more available there is always going to be a need for marketplaces to form to organize that information from these markets. Anytime there is a marketplace, there will be scope for dynamic pricing, in turn. In fact, some people like Dan Leahy have organized marketplaces specifically to do dynamic pricing. This is also, what Aaron and I have done through our startup Dynos. Dynos allows restaurants to list time-specific discounts so that they can offer discounts at times when they are empty. This allows them to specifically speed up their traditionally slow times. In Dynos, we've built a marketplace where everyday restaurants can join one platform where their price levels are displayed. If a restaurant is offering a discount, then on the Dynos app the discount available for that respective restaurant near you is displayed as soon as you open the app.

The thing about marketplaces is that while they have massive potential to benefit consumers and producers by organizing the information in the market about prices and goods, marketplaces are super tough to build. Just ask me and Aaron, we've been building a marketplace for restaurants for our startup Dynos. Marketplaces are tough to build because all businesses are only as strong as the network that upholds them. For traditional, "I'm just selling you [insert good here]" businesses, the network that matters is the customer base. For example, all that matters to Chipotle is making sure that avid Chipotle fans keep coming and their ranks keep growing.

The thing about marketplaces is that you have to not only have a really strong network of customers but also have a great network of service providers. This is to say that Uber is a very good marketplace for ride-sharing because it has a lot of customers but also because it has a lot of drivers with cars. Importantly, those two things are quite interrelated. You won't get any customers if you don't have providers, and you won't get providers if you don't have any customers. So when you're starting at zero like Dynos did, that puts everyone in a very tough position.

Being part of a startup in its initial phases is loads of fun. Everything is happening at once, and you have to build up a way of dealing with the responsibilities and demands of the business. One of the major demands of any business is acquiring customers.

During some of the very first days of Dynos, we were finally moving into the beta-test phase. In other words, our app was soon becoming available to a very limited subset of testers. In order get people to sign up to test the app, Aaron and I decided to put up fliers all over Georgetown's campus.

My co-founder Aaron is a bit obsessive. In the course of flyers being stuck to walls, there are going to be instances where they come down. Maybe a janitor takes one down accidentally, maybe the wind blows one off a wall outdoors or maybe some prick thinks it's funny to rip one off the wall. Aaron was personally offended every time he noticed there was no longer a flyer where one once was. Eventually, Aaron noticed some specific locations where the flyers kept coming down. He started a shadowboxing campaign against whatever force was bringing the flyers down.

One specific battlefield was the lobby of our dorm, Arrupe hall. Aaron would walk in every day, and the fliers would be gone, and he would go berserk. He would go upstairs to our room, grab another copy, and bring it down. Every time a flyer came down, it went back up. Every time it went up, it came back down. Eventually, Aaron decided to strike punitively. He put up three fliers one day. The next he put up four, once the three came down. This dance went on for days. Eventually, the mystery force gave up. He allowed one flier to remain in the Arrupe lobby, and ever since then there has been a detente.

This story is marginal. It is not very broadly applicable. But it symbolizes something that is none of those things. What this story really symbolizes is that it's hard to build a marketplace. It's hard to get customers to join, usually for the simple reason that you do not yet have a network of vendors to give them quality service yet. However, this is also true for structural, individual, and sometimes silly reasons, as this story illustrates.

Dan Leahy, the former-CEO of Savored- a site which allowed people to book time sensitive reservations at discounted prices for high-end restaurants, faced this exact same problem.

Dan came at the issue with his own perspective. Before he founded Savored he spent a few years in investment banking. He couldn't stand it, he needed to do something else, anything else. So he and a former classmate of his quit their jobs and founded Savored.

Dan broke the problem into two parts-

The first problem was the consumer side. Starting from zero, it is always incredibly important to deviate from that number. It is even more important to do it quickly. So, Dan focused on the consumers he knew he could get. Before the site even launched, Dan created a sort of waitlist. On it, Dan tried to sign up as many people as possible. He told friends from college and high school, family, coworkers, anyone, who would listen, about the idea.

But his appeal went beyond just asking people he knew to support him. If he had just done that, perhaps far fewer people would have signed up at all. Instead, and interestingly, he tried to sell potential customers on the dream of eating out at fancy places. He sold them on the idea that they could achieve a status while still saving. In the way, he positioned and sold his product he isolated the very core of why higher-end restaurants exist.

Every person has an idea of where they'd want their life to go in the best case scenario. For some of us, that means imagining ourselves in the Oval Office, the C-Suite or the Box Office. All of us have deep-seated—while unrealistic—dreams of a more sophisticated life. Part of that story inevitably includes fine dining. From the CEO having a high-powered dinner with business partners to politicians hammering out a deal over dinner, there is already a connection in people's minds between high-end food and success. Dan connected that story to his company. His message was basically that celebrities eat here, and you can too.

Ultimately, if you're building a marketplace from scratch, you need to connect to people more deeply. Because if you don't have a compelling and resonant reason for why people should actively spend energy to join something that has not yet been established, then they simply will not. In the same way, revolutions are built on an idea, so too are marketplaces. As Dan explained, "we found that customers were willing to dine at different times given the proper incentive, and that is kind of how it all got started."

Dan framed his product in a way that connected with users. That is how he built up a baseline on one side of the marketplace and got them to be patient enough to wait for it to come out.

The second problem then was the supply side. Dan explained how restaurant owners were primarily concerned with two things. Firstly, obviously, they wanted to know that the economics of it all made sense. Dan explained how they could make a ton of money during times when they were simply wasting their own potential. Secondly, they were concerned that by giving out discounts they would somehow lower the prestige of their service to their broader customer base. In this sense, the restaurants were concerned about winning the battle but losing the war, so to speak. On this more nuanced concern, Dan explained how the service would remain tremendously discrete.

Again, Dan sold the dream of greatly increased revenue to these venues, even at times when it wasn't certain. As it was not certain at the beginning.

It became far easier, once greatly increased revenue became a reality for some restaurants that did join the network. For example, at almost every new city in which Savored arrived, Dan needed to build a new network from scratch. But, it was easier and easier with each successive city because he could point to examples like Kiddie Chai, a hip Thai restaurant in New York, where implementing Savored directly led to tens of thousands of dollars of incremental revenue a month.

If one thing is clear, building nascent networks are perceptual battles. How do you convince two sets of neutrals to join your side? How do you frame your story to meet what your customers and providers want to hear?

People like Dan Leahy, companies like Zaarly, and startups like Dynos are doing the heavy lifting of building these marketplaces. These marketplaces were made possible and necessary by technological shifts because you can't aggregate all the information in one place without the incredibly quick transmission of information that is made possible by the internet, or without the uniquity of access to devices that can receive that information. In turn, these marketplaces have actively made dynamic pricing cheap and effective both for businesses that need no longer change physical price tags and for consumers who can, quickly and freely, get the information they need in one place within a few clicks on a phone.

CHAPTER 3

CULTURAL SHIFTS

———

There's a lot of retail stores that change or revamp their prices every quarter as some styles fall out of favor with consumers. Is anyone really opposed to that? Most grocery stores increase the price of Strawberries in the winter when the supply of Strawberries are low. Is anyone really opposed to that? Stock prices for every public company fluctuate up and down throughout the day. Is anyone really opposed to that?

If you're not opposed to any of these types of price changes, then you support price changes over time based on demand fluctuations generally. The only difference between those examples and how Uber prices, is that the price changes are done faster when its Uber. But what is the philosophical difference? After all, a price change is a price change, where is the meaningful philosophical bright line between price changes once every six months and once every second? How can people support the principles behind dynamic pricing, but oppose dynamic pricing?

Still, there are plenty of people who say that they are categorically opposed to dynamic pricing. We've already seen this with Coca-Cola, where the plan to dynamically price vending machines was retracted because of consumer uproar. It's important to realize that any time there is a new idea, there is always some backlash to the idea, simply because it is a deviation from the way things used to be done. This opposition to dynamic pricing, specifically, needs to be overcome, for dynamic pricing to maximally impact the economy and society. How can skeptics be convinced?

In 1954, Gordon Allport put forward a concept called contact theory. His premise was simple. The more an individual person interacted with different types of people, the less prejudice he would have towards those different types of people (Allport). While this theory has been applied from everything from school integration to sports teams, the broad foundational principle has always been the same: the more a person interacts with someone else the more he likes that other person.

Similarly, the shift in cultural norms and attitudes in favor of dynamic pricing in the status quo is being spurred on by a form of what I've started to call "pricing contact theory". In other words, as people interact more and more with the idea of dynamic pricing, they become less opposed to it. Just take a look at dynamic pricing in baseball.

Imagine that you were planning on going to your local MLB team's baseball game this weekend. Imagine, that there was a 60% chance of rain. What if you take the risk, go to the game, and it does rain. Wouldn't you feel like you should have been charged less? Would it be fair for you to be charged the same amount as someone who bought tickets for the same seats on a different weekend when there was no chance of rain?

One of my good friends, Arnav, played Little League in third grade. One time, his coach, who had season tickets for the Nationals, saw that the weather report indicated it was going to rain. Losing his appetite, the coach gave away those tickets to Arnav and Arnav's father for the weekend. So Arnav and his father went to the game. As soon as they got to their seats, it started raining almost immediately. Arnav sat there for hours miserably getting soaked and feeling cold in his core. After two hours, he asked his dad, "Can we please leave?" His dad said, "Wait. The game is almost over." After five minutes, Arnav grew impatient, so he asked again, "Can we go?" His dad responded again, "We're almost done." Arnav lost it. He started nagging his dad, constantly asking him if they could leave. Eventually, his dad gave in, and they went home without staying until the end, deeply unsatisfied. Now imagine if they'd had to pay for those tickets. In fact, imagine if they'd been forced to pay the same price that someone who watched the same game on a beautiful day would've paid. Does that seem fair?

When the global economy melted in 2008, the effects ravaged every sector of the American economy. In the aftermath, entire industries changed forever. They were forced to innovate to survive. One market that, perhaps under the radar, was revolutionized by the consequences of the meltdown was Major League Baseball. In 2009, as jobs were being destroyed, and incomes were sliding downwards, many Major League Baseball teams decided to reduce ticket prices in order to maintain sales since families were less likely to prioritize spending money out of a shrinking budget on Baseball tickets.

That same year, instead of simply slashing ticket prices, the San Francisco Giants decided to try something that no team had ever done in Major League Baseball. They ran a simple experiment. They budgeted a mere 2000 seats in the behemoth AT&T stadium for a trial revenue management dynamic pricing scheme. Over the course of 2009, they generated an extra $500, 000 in revenue from those seats. In 2010, they implemented revenue management dynamic pricing stadium-wide.

Why did this work so effectively? Firstly, stadium seats are a perishable good. If a team does not sell tickets by the 1st pitch of the game, then they get nothing at all. Therefore, moving tickets before that time through dynamic changes is more important than small changes in the margin. Secondly, demand for tickets fluctuates widely. If the weather is good, or the team has won a lot of games in a row, people want tickets a lot more than in the respective counterfactuals where the weather is bad or teams have losing streaks. As Russ Stanley explains, "A Monday Pirates game is not going to be the same as a Dodger Sunday, so pricing them the same way doesn't make a whole lot of sense." (Overby). Lastly, there is a rather large fixed inventory at the AT&T stadium, while the variable costs of printing and allocating another ticket is quite low. These factors come together to make dynamic pricing successful for this market, just as it has been successful for movie tickets, Broadway shows, and concerts.

On the surface, the public backlash could be catastrophic if fans became upset with the new policies. Fans could boycott games, generating lower revenue and negative press, while harming the morale of the team. Due to this, the Giants took on great risk by boldly moving into territory that other franchises were afraid to do. This is even more true, given that these decisions were made in the shadow of the greatest economic recession since the Great Depression.

Yet how did they prevent the kind of backlash that forced Coca-Cola to reverse its position on dynamic pricing in 1999? After all, there are a lot of potential eggshells in implementing this idea. Season ticket holders could become upset when prices became cheaper for seats that they paid more for. Uncertainty about ticket prices going up and down could prevent some purchases and cause people to regret the purchases they do make. At the end of the day, any time a bold decision is made like this one, the status quo will be changed and so there inevitably will be some disagreement and backlash because it flies in the face of tradition. What was surprising in this case was how marginal it was in scope and magnitude, and the reason why became clear to me last summer.

I'm a massive Manchester United fan. Growing up, I would wake up at 7 am on Saturdays to watch them play soccer on TV. Imagine a ten-year-old kid voluntarily getting up at 7 am, when was the last time that happened? Manchester United meant the world to me. All I wanted was to see the players live. Last summer, Manchester United granted my wish. They came to the United States to play a friendly match against Barcelona in Washington DC. I was beyond ecstatic, it transported me back to my childhood in a deep nostalgic way. In fact, I organized my travel plans around this singular event. However, despite meticulous planning and carefully researched decision making in every other stage of preparing for this event, when it came time to buy tickets, I didn't even check two different websites. I went straight to StubHub, unconsciously. This game was tremendously important to me, and still, I didn't even think twice. As this story shows, for many people in my generation, buying tickets online for everything from movies to matches has become embedded in the way we act. What, in economics, is referred to as a secondary market of resales has become *our* primary market for purchasing.

In the case of the Giants, it turns out that fans, like those in my generation, had slowly over the years become culturally more accustomed to this idea of varying ticket prices. The underlying cause of this cultural shift was these e-commerce sites like StubHub that operated a secondary market for tickets. On StubHub, people who already have tickets are selling them to people who do not. Simple supply and demand set the price on that website, not the Stadium ticket office. So slowly, but surely, people have become more and more accustomed to different prices, ones determined by the secondary market for these tickets and others by the primary market where teams used to set their own prices at some fixed number. "StubHub has enabled dynamic pricing," claims Barry Kahn the CEO of Qcue, a dynamic pricing firm (Sachdev). Over the years there have been smaller steps of backlash which were swept away in waves of cultural change. By the time the Giants introduced this bold new policy. To consumers, It wasn't all that bold and it wasn't all that new. It was just an extension of an underlying trend in the secondary market that now moved into the primary market.

What does the Giant's experience teach us? I think ultimately what it tells us is that what is considered fair is arbitrary. In fact, it's just a matter of perception. The way to avoid getting tripped up by perception, in turn, is nothing more than making people feel like something is normal. It's a matter of socializing consumers in how you do business. If you've grown up believing that prices will be static and that is fair, then that's what you'll think is fair. However, if you've grown-up like I have surrounded by new technologies like Uber, Lyft, StubHub, and Priceline, dynamic prices feel intuitive. They just feel like something we've always done, why would we do it any other way?

That's the concept behind pricing contact theory. As the former-CTO of Priceline, Scott Case, explains, the key is exposure. He said "when I use Uber three times a week, I'm exposed to that more. If grocery store prices were fluctuating day to day, and I could see that happening, I would be more exposed to that; therefore, I might have a better understanding of that." In other words, if exposure is increased, acceptance will increase too.

When it comes to converting people who consider fixed prices to be normal, I think the Giants lay out a great play. Ease them in. StubHub opened the door, and then the Giants dynamically pricing based on supply and demand felt normal. In fact, to consumers, it began to actively make sense to reconcile the primary and secondary markets by floating prices.

Therefore, the way to manage backlash, it to take a little on at a time, instead of a lot at once. Ease them in, and explain each step along the way. If you have a good economic argument, that truly benefits the community, eventually, people will hear it out. Slowly but surely people will start to accept it and that's how norms change. Now is the perfect time to transition. People are feeling these shifts all around them. Transportation, energy, entertainment, and retail, everything is slowly changing. As they get eased in, as their norms change, consumers can finally give way to the light.

Today, the overwhelming majority of the MLB utilize dynamic pricing. The Giants were the first across the bridge, and now everyone else has stampeded across.

Looking into the future, where dynamic pricing is least likely to provoke a backlash, we are probably going to see it adopted quickly. One particular example is the restaurant industry.

Its a simple fact of life that happiness and unhappiness lie in the gap between expectations and reality. We are overwhelmed with joy when someone throws us a surprise party, and we are tremendously upset when a movie doesn't live up to its glowing reviews. Dynamic pricing, therefore, occupies a precarious place in the spectrum of human happiness. On the one hand, we love when our Ubers are cheaper than our usual fare. On the other, we are very distraught when the app is surging the price. Sometimes, due to negativity bias, humans overweight those negative experiences and condemn the entirety of the practice itself. This is wrong of us, and slowly the cultural norms are shifting away from this worldview.

Irrespective, when you're trying to build a business, you can't expect the world to conform to what you think is right, you have to recognize perceptions as they already are, even if they are changing. In the status-quo, a lot of people are upset when prices go up. Sometimes, this leads to public backlash that can condemn a brand. When Aaron and I were exploring the scope for dynamic pricing in a wide variety of industries, we realized that the restaurant space was unique. Here was a place where demand fluctuated sharply throughout the day, and quite often shifting prices downwards would be the more profitable move.

This is for a few simple reasons. Firstly, restaurants have high fixed costs, they've already paid for rent, electricity, labor, and the food. If they don't generate revenue throughout the day, all of that investment is wasted. Secondly, often inventory at restaurants is perishable, if they don't sell it, they throw it away. Because of these factors, restaurants would rather take a lower margin on the food they might otherwise throw away, rather than a total loss. Dan Leahy, the former-CEO of Savored, confirmed this. Speaking about when he was setting up to start his own company, he said, "very uneven demand patterns really plagued places like restaurants and spas and places with high fixed costs but low variable costs." Evaluating this landscape, my own solution was simple restaurants ought to price downwards at off-peak hours. This would increase traffic to stores when they would otherwise be empty and would allow restaurants to offload excess inventory at some margin, as opposed to no margin.

This all makes sense on paper, but how could we be sure to avoid the backlash that so many companies have felt? After all, jealousy is a powerful thing. Even if the individuals themselves were better off because prices were cheaper at specific times, and never above list price at others, wouldn't the people paying list price feel like they were cheated? Also, wouldn't expectations adjust downwards over time?

To contextualize this, imagine a person going to a restaurant two days in a row. If on his first time he pays $7 for a sandwich because the store is empty and on his second he pays $10 for the same sandwich because the store is busy, wouldn't he feel upset that he had to pay more? Aaron and I posited that he would not. Firstly, framing is very important in how expectations are created, and if framed in the right way dynamic pricing can prevent these expectation shifts. If the $7 sandwich was framed as a deviation from the norm of $10, then people's baseline expectation would remain at $10. Any decrease from that baseline would cause happiness, but staying at it would just be seen as a resumption of the status quo. Secondly, if the $3 saving meant that much to the customer, over time he could adjust his eating habits to make sure he only ate at off-peak hours. At least now he would have the option to save money, as opposed to being condemned to paying $10 all the time. Both of these things, minimized backlash risk significantly in this market.

Given the economic opportunity and the minimization of backlash risk, we saw restaurants as a tremendous opportunity. So Aaron and I launched Dynos, a company dedicated to making restaurants more efficient and profitable by implementing dynamic pricing and making customers happier by decreasing their prices at off-peak hours. By targeting this specific market, we avoided the pitfalls of backlash, because we only coopted many of the aspects of dynamic pricing that made people happier, by allowing them to afford things at a cheaper price, instead of surging to increase revenue as many other markets would require.

As the low-hanging fruit of low backlash markets like restaurants is picked off, more and more contact with dynamic pricing will continue to shift consumer sentiment towards the practice. Adoption in how we watch sports and eat food, in turn, will be likely to acclimate people to this new form of pricing, priming them in-case other markets follow and decide to also implement dynamic pricing. Therefore, more dynamic pricing in one industry might lead to more dynamic pricing in another industry. Eventually, dynamic pricing will reach a tipping point, where it explodes into every market. We are soon approaching that moment.

CHAPTER 4

WHAT IS A PRICE REALLY?

———

Jackie Mason once said, "Money isn't the most important thing in the world. Love is. Fortunately, I love money." That joke is so clever, precisely because he uses two different meanings of the word money, in one sentence. The first meaning is money as a currency in itself. The second is what the money can buy.

A few weeks ago, I was at a charity event called "Night of Too Many Stars." The purpose of the event was to raise money for an autism charity, a noble cause by any measure. As I sat in my seat, item after item was auctioned off at the event. A night out with Jon Stewart, dinner with both Matt Damon and Jimmy Kimmel, and so on were all auctioned, selling for tens of thousands or even hundreds of thousands of dollars. As I sat in my seat, I felt like raising my hand every time an item came up during the auction—even for items I didn't particularly want. Of course, I never did, but I felt an odd, strong desire to just put it all on the table. It was at that moment that I realized that Jackie Mason was onto something. Too often, what money is and what it represents get conflated.

Consider this example. The most expensive watch to sell at an auction, to date, is a Daytona Rolex formerly owned by Paul Newman (Wolf). The watch was auctioned by Phillips Auction House, and after an intense 12-minute bidding war, the watch was sold (Wolf). It sold for almost $18 million dollars (Wolf). It's truly not my place to say, and maybe my opinion is wrong, but I find it remarkable that someone can be simultaneously smart enough to build a massive fortune and dumb enough to spend $18 million dollars on a watch. Whenever I see a headline like that, I get annoyed. Yet, there is a distinction to be made about why. I'm not upset because someone spent $18 million dollars on a watch. I'm upset because they could have spent that money on literally anything else. You might say, well isn't that the same thing? What does a $18 million dollar price tag mean? For that matter, what does any price tag mean?

That brings us the the most baseline economic question of all. What is a price really? After all, I can't eat a bank account or watch Netflix on a dollar bill. What I lose when I buy a $20 movie ticket, isn't really the $20 bill, but rather I lose what else I could have bought with that bill. In other words, for the consumer, the price of something is what economists call the opportunity cost. For example, if I spend $20 on a movie ticket, that's $20 fewer dollars that I can spend on drinks at a bar. It's also $20 fewer dollars than I can spend on an $18 million dollar watch. For the producer, the price is what they are willing to get, in exchange for their product. Ultimately, every producer only wants revenue, so that he or she can also consume.

Ok, all of that is fairly obvious, what does any of that have to do with dynamic pricing? Ultimately, you cannot understand shifts in pricing, unless you understand pricing. Moreover, you cannot understand what a price is unless you can understand how prices are denominated. To comprehensively understand how dynamic pricing is going to effect the economy, therefore, one must also have an overall understanding of how economic exchanges occur.

To begin, lets consider currency. We have currency because barter systems rely on a mutual coincidence of wants. To illustrate, let's pretend that I produce apples and I want a car. In the absence of some currency, a medium of exchange, I would have to trade some massive amount of apples for a car. The issue is, I would have to find a car owner or dealer who wants that many apples or any apples at all. This creates a lot of friction in the economy because now I have to go around looking for a car seller with a massive appetite for apples. There is a simple solution to this problem, societies create currencies and denominate prices in those currencies. Now I can sell my apples in the market for dollars, and use those dollars to buy a car or anything else I'd like. This general concept first introduced itself to me in the fourth grade.

In the fourth grade, at the tender age of ten, I became a massive Pokémon fan. One of my friends got a Nintendo Gameboy and a game called Pokémon Emerald. We would sit around the lunch table every day, and play on his Gameboy, training these virtual creatures in an attempt to be the best. Eventually, we moved away from the digital and into the physical. We started collecting and trading Pokémon cards, cards with our favorite creatures displayed on them. Every day during lunch, the cafeteria would transform into a commercial hub of trading activity. As we sipped on our chocolate milk, we were busy trying to extract rare and coveted Pokémon cards from people who had them in exchange for cards we currently possessed.

Not every card was valued the same. Some had a Pokémon that I loved. Others had Pokémon that my friends liked more. Additionally, all Pokémon cards varied in their level of scarcity. Some Pokémon cards were super common. Others we could only whisper about because no one had them.

Given the circumstances, as a nascent Pokémon card collector, the objective was to acquire as many of the rare cards, especially those with Pokémon characters that I individually adored. Back when I was in the trading game, the card that met both of these requirements for me was the Charizard EX card. Charizard EX was not only a super rare card, but it also had my favorite Pokémon- Charizard. Everyone in my school wanted one. Luckily for us, there was a kid in my school who had one. Being a deal maker, I was hopeful that one day I could make a deal with the kid for his card.

One day, I approached the kid during lunch in an attempt to monitor his temperature with regards to a deal. I asked him, "what do you want in in exchange for the Charizard EX." He responded with the most outrageous laundry list of cards. Cards that would take weeks, maybe even months, of trading for me to acquire. Thus began my trading journey.

As I started trading more and more, I learned other children's card preferences and negotiation styles. I learned how to get deals with some stubborn kids by making intermediary trades with someone else to acquire what they really wanted. Eventually, word spread that I was putting together a package of cards to trade for the Charizard EX card. With them knowing this, I had a much more difficult time acquiring the last half of the laundry list. The other kids I was dealing with knew I needed what they had to get what I wanted. They would drive incredibly tough bargains and knew I would have to capitulate to get what I wanted.

Since there was no objective unit of account, each card's "price" was denominated in the minds of people I was bartering with. As such, "prices" were constantly in flux, as I would offer different types of cards and sets of cards to potential traders. Any potential trading partner's willingness to do a deal was entirely based on his or her subjective valuation of how valuable their cards were and how valuable what I was offering was.

As such, there were a lot of opportunities for arbitrage. You could find some kids who valued some cards more than others, and by trading around, you could leave everyone better off in terms of each person's evaluation of the value of his or her deck.

During the course of trading, something interesting started to happen. A really common card was the energy card. It didn't have a Pokémon on it at all, it just said energy. None of knew what to do with this card, and it served no purpose for us. Organically, during the course of my trading, some kids started using energy cards as a form of currency. They would "price" their Pokémon cards with characters at X number of energy cards. That way, energy cards became a medium of exchange- a currency. This was super helpful, now instead of having to do a ton of intermediate exchanges until the mutual wants lined up. I could just get enough energy cards and trade straight up.

I worked really hard to cobble enough of the right cards together. Eventually, after nearly a month, I assembled this deck that the owner of the Charizard EX wanted in exchange. Finally, I arrived at the cafeteria one day with the entirety of the deck that the owner of the Charizard EX had outlined as his price for a trade, and he said to me, "I don't know if I want to trade anymore." He delineated some more cards he wanted. I was livid.

I said firmly, "no." I continued, "my offer is take it or leave it." Frankly, if he had responded by saying that he would leave it, I probably would have gone back to trading to get those extra cards. However, he crumbled under the pressure and took the deal.

What can this simple story about 4th graders in a Cafeteria teach you a lot about currencies?

Firstly, currencies are incredibly helpful in speeding up exchanges of goods. When instead of finding the exact cards that someone wanted in exchange for other cards, I could just trade in terms of something common that everyone had, transaction speed rocketed.

Secondly, currencies are helpful in terms of serving as a unit of account. If someone says that he would accept 5 energy cards for a specific Pokémon card. That gives me a clearer view of the "price" than if he lists other cards of equal worth, for which subjective preferences are more arbitrary.

Lastly, currencies can be very unstable. If for example, some kids just bought a lot of energy cards, now knowing that energy cards are a common medium, then the currency would collapse, because there would be a massive influx of that card into the market, and anything worth 5 energy cards, would have to increase to 50 energy cards, or else it would be devalued.

How do these facts, and the story generally, relate to shifts in pricing and shifts in technology taking place right now?

Firstly, dynamic pricing can better account for environments where inflation or deflation or other currency instability is rocking the economy. For example, when Zimbabwe's currency began hyperinflating, if all pricing was done dynamically, then the day to day increases in the price, indexed to inflation changes, could help sellers continue to get fair prices for their goods. While this doesn't solve the larger problem of the currency itself rapidly approaching worthlessness and wiping out people's savings, it would be an improvement over having to shut down because the normal prices simply make business unsustainable.

Secondly, coordinating between different currencies. Every day cryptocurrencies gain increasing acceptance and increasingly are used for day to day transactions. Perhaps then, dynamic pricing can index the various fluctuations in dollar valuations for cryptocurrencies and set the prices for any respective cryptocurrency accordingly. This can help make cryptocurrencies more liquid, while also benefiting businesses.

Thirdly, dynamic pricing on a mass scale will influence how consumers decide to make tradeoffs. When prices were fixed, it was much easier to quantify opportunity costs from a consumer's perspective. For example, if a movie ticket is always $20, it is easier for me to realize that spending $20 on a new pair of headphones directly trades-off with my ability to purchase tickets for a date at the movies. However, when prices fluctuate in markets, such as constantly changing ticket prices, those tradeoffs become less clear. As a result, consumers will have to start thinking more broadly in opportunity cost ranges, as opposed to fixed tradeoffs. Extending the previous example, this would look like me realizing that buying that same $20 pair of headphones would tradeoff with anywhere from 1 to 3 movie tickets, depending on when I make that purchase for movie tickets. This process will occur naturally, but it is a substantial shift in how consumers are used to making decisions in the status quo. Savvy consumers today can get a leg up on making smart purchasing decisions by understanding this basic fact. By changing the way they think now, they can be better prepared and able to decide whether or not any given purchase is right for them by evaluating the range of possible tradeoffs.

Lastly, while we might think that we have moved away from negotiations like the ones I had to do in that elementary school cafeteria, with the digitalization of commerce and the embracement of dynamic pricing schemes, transactions might become more about negotiations again. Negotiating will probably never return to the art of the past between people engaged in a battle of wills. Instead, implicit negotiating, where customers don't buy until prices dip to certain levels, will emerge. Furthermore, tools like "name your own price" by Priceline, and auction markets like those created by eBay, are increasingly reintroducing negotiations. Increasingly, consumer tools, that utilize algorithms to figure out how to beat strategies employed by producers, will emerge to counter the power of producers in these negotiations by informing users what price they should be willing to pay in order to maximize their own welfare.

Once you understand what a price really is, it becomes clear that adapting to a new dynamic pricing landscape is increasingly required. We've developed habits of thinking about purchasing decisions that are not necessarily compatible with the way pricing is moving in the future. It is contingent on us to realize those archaic habits and change the way we consume.

Whether this is anticipating price drops for a given good in the near future and then waiting to buy that item until then or actually comprehending how much we could be giving up by thinking in ranges, consumption behaviors must and will change. This sort of shift in mindset is also true of business practices that use dynamic pricing to better adapt to changing currencies and other market factors.

CHAPTER 5

A BASIC ECONOMIC FRAMEWORK OF PRICES

———

John Maynard Keynes, one of the great economists in history, famously proclaimed, "In the long run, we are all dead." While a bit nihilistic and morbid, there is great wisdom in that statement. In our quest to explain how the world works, economists talk about things like long run and short run, seemingly blind to all the assumptions they make. One of those assumptions is that any of this matters after your life ends. While you're chewing on that food for thought, consider another useful—but perhaps imperfect—economic assumption: the rationality of consumers.

You don't need a Ph.D. in economics to come to the conclusion that the cheaper something is the more people will want it and the more expensive that product becomes, the fewer people will demand it. But the people who do have PhDs agree with you, in almost all cases.

In mainstream economic thought, it is assumed that people are rational. Economists explain that people have budget constraints like the amount of waking hours they have to live or the amount of money they have to spend, and then they make decisions to spend that limited amount of time or money on things that can maximize their expected satisfaction. This is the reason that when prices for an item decrease the quantity demanded of that item increases because people recalculate how much their income can buy them and how they want to budget their income with regards to spending on various products.

Often times in introductory economics textbooks, demand is described solely as a function of price. The reason dynamic pricing, or any type of pricing change works, then, is because different prices correspond to different quantities of demand. If demand is weak, you can boost it by decreasing prices. This mental model, while imperfect, is not wholly inaccurate. In fact, McDonald's seems to have mastered this strategy.

Over the last few years, McDonald's has introduced a dollar price menu, brought back cheap, all-day breakfast and decreased prices on various items. Why? The people in charge of pricing at McDonald's working off of intuitions about what motivates customers, economic predictions and empirical evidence decided that when prices go down, demand goes up. In 2017, they decided to crater costs on drinks. As Jack Russo from Edward D. Jones & Co. explained at the time, "Demand has been a little weak." (Patton). He further asserted, "A lot of these guys think they've got to keep promoting to keep people coming in the door." (Patton).

While demand can be manipulated by price changes, it is also important to note that the amount demand changes depends on how elastic or price-sensitive people's demands are. In some markets, even a big change in price won't change demand that much. In others, a small change in price will totally skew the quantity demanded.

It is against this backdrop of consumer behavior that dynamic pricing is studied in most academic settings. Definitionally, dynamic pricing encompasses a whole range of pricing strategies. Primarily there are four.

1.   There is fixed-rules dynamic pricing.
2.   There is conditional-rules dynamic pricing.
3.   There is revenue management.
4.   There is personalized pricing or perfect price discrimination.

In turn, there is a subsequent chapter in this book devoted to each respective main category of dynamic pricing. In those chapters we'll take a look at how those strategies fare in the real world. However, to understand the conceptual underpinnings behind these pricing strategies, we're going to conduct a thought experiment on the busy streets of Morocco in this chapter.

Place yourself within the scene. You're the owner of a bazaar shop in the streets of Casablanca, Morocco. The city's geography, located on the Mediterranean, endows it with a distinctive diversity as a broad range of people, of every shade and story, meet on those streets, exchanging culture, contacts, and coin.

On this particular day, in late Spring, the weather is perfect. The streets are teeming with people. Shop owners, just like you, sit at their own stands, which surround both sides of the narrow path. Your stand's main products are ceramic plates with intricate geometric designs and colors. These designs and colors interact in truly vibrant and unique ways, ways that go beyond the realm of cutlery and into the realm of art. You're selling these plates with intricate designs to everyone and anyone who walks through those streets, as are tens of other shopkeepers located on your street.

Your shop is a humble institution. A small and sturdy stand in the midst of others. As you sit in that stand your focus is singular: you need customers not only to approach and purchase your goods but also to purchase your goods in a way that maximizes your profits. The question then is simple:

what is your strategy? There is an innumerable number of ways that you can determine what exactly to set your prices at. Against the backdrop of Casablanca's beautiful winding roads, let's compare a few of them.

Let's say you start the week with a strategy called cost-plus. This is a fixed price strategy that takes whatever it cost you to produce the good, and tacks on a margin on top. For the sake of argument, let us say that the cost and margin combined to leave you with a fixed price of 70 Moroccan dirhams per unit. You put up a large chalkboard in the front of your stand, and you write a massive numerical "seventy" on that board, publically signaling to everyone in your small little world what your policy is going to be. For the sake of illustration, let's say that you actually commit to such a strategy. No matter who walks through the street and how hard they try to negotiate, that is the price you will sell one of your painted plates at— take it or leave it. Of the roughly thousand people that walk through, many see the price listed and stop by to check the merchandise. Strangely, very few of them buy your plates. Why? You later see them go to the competing stands and buy plates there. What is going on?

Maybe the price is too high. So the next day, you lower it to 60 Moroccan dirhams per unit. You erase your chalkboard. In its place, you write a massive numerical "sixty" in a bigger bolder typeface. Smuggly at the beginning of the day, you expect your sales to increase. Shockingly, while slightly more people stop and come to your stall to see your merchandise, very few plates are sold. The situation is turning precarious. What is going on?

The free market throws each participant into a brutal state of nature, one where each actor is not only more than willing to put you to the sword but is actively encouraged to do so.

What is going on is that customers are checking out your prices and then going to other stands, where competing shop owners are priced at a far lower value. They've been selling at 50 Moroccan dirhams per unit. Accordingly, people, being rational, have flocked to your competitors. It turns out that your competitors, have been undercutting you. Now, if you stay on this course of action it is incredibly unlikely that you make it through the summer. You need to adapt or die. It seems you have one rather clear option. You have to fight fire with fire.

On the third day, you decide to use a dynamic pricing strategy instead of the simple cost-plus, that you'd committed to before. You erase the chalkboard, and instead of writing a price, you write in bold letters- "will match, and go slightly lower than, any price!" Your competitors, realize the futility of going lower in prices now that you will match them. Not knowing what else to do, and hoping brand loyalty and "superior" quality will protect their customer base, they decide to stick with their price of 50 Moroccan dirhams per unit.

This idea of price-matching is a conditional rule-based form of dynamic pricing. Under this paradigm, certain things need to happen, for prices to be dynamic, otherwise, they are fixed. In this example, if your competitors stay at your prices, your prices are fixed. If they change their prices, your prices dynamically adjust downwards.

Going from customers consistently giving you the cold shoulder, magnitudes more are now coming up to you and telling what they were quoted at other places. As you match those prices and go slightly lower yourself, they decide to buy from you. Profits skyrocket. Yes, your price at each sale is strictly lower, but the higher volume of sales more than makes up for it.

Suddenly, mission creep kicks in. Realizing the power of dynamic pricing, you think that you can do even better.

Up to this point, all dynamic pricing changes were made based on what other producers were charging. But, now you decide to factor in how demand changes too. You've noticed that your store is significantly less busy on Thursdays, for whatever reason. What is there to be done about that?

On the fourth day, you wipe the chalkboard again and write "will offer a special discount on Thursdays". Word spreads to local consumers that there is going to be a massive sale on Thursday. All of a sudden, Thursday rolls around, and it's your busiest day of the week yet! This is fixed-rules dynamic pricing. In this paradigm, a fixed rule like special discounts on certain days is set. Then, regardless of other market conditions, prices adjust according to the rule, in this case they go down on every Thursday.

By the fifth day, you've driven your competitors to the brink. You decide to put them to the sword. Now you choose to determine your prices based on the number of certain plates you have left, combined with how much in demand they are. Above all, you want to make sure to sell the plates, before the designs go out of style. Based on how busy the store is throughout the day, combined with how much inventory you have, you change prices throughout the day. Prices go up when there is a lot of demand. As prices go up during these peak demand period, you make more money per sale. As prices go down when there is little demand, more people come to buy things, and this makes you more money. Overall, by offering special discounts on items before they go out of style, you get rid of all of your perishable goods.

This form of dynamic pricing is called revenue-management. As we will analyze in far greater detail later, this is the sort of dynamic pricing that companies like Uber, Priceline, and Lyft have mastered. Due to leaps in technology, this is the form of dynamic pricing that has become most effective in maximizing revenue.

On that same day, your competitors cannot take it anymore. They decide to switch away from their decision to have fixed prices. They instead buy whiteboards and all of them write "will match any price!" Unfortunately, this will be their downfall.

Because of their strategy, which you have decided to match, there is a massive race to the bottom. Because of this race to the bottom, the prices charged at each store go all the way down to the marginal cost it took to produce that specific unit. A lot of your competitors just cannot survive, because their costs of production are higher than yours. Instead of making greater losses, they sell their shops to you and drop out of the market.

On the sixth day- something painfully obvious becomes clearer. You realize that you can charge different people different prices. After all, it is not like they can go to other stores, you own them all! Furthermore, in this wonderfully diverse city, there are many types of people, from European tourists to local house-keepers. For each person, you start quoting a different price. You start charging wealthy families visiting from London and Paris, more than you charge Moroccan looking families. These tourists are more likely to pay more since they have more money generally and far less likely to go to your competitors to haggle because they only have so much time in Morocco. All of a sudden, you make more and more money.

This is personalized pricing. Under this paradigm, the producer tries to extract as much revenue as possible out of each and every person. A certain level of monopoly power and information about consumer habits are required to do this type of pricing effectively.

On the seventh day, you decide to retire. After all, you had a great run. Now its time to relax on the boat you just bought with all of your profits.

The big takeaway from this thought experiment is that in certain markets, with different types of customers, some strategies work way better than others. Hopefully, you can now see how a plethora of strategies work, how competitors can sometimes respond to them, and how equilibriums can form. These are all ideas we will delve deeper into in the following chapters.

CHAPTER 6

HOW PRICES ARE PERCEIVED

———

There's a scene in *The Dark Knight*, where Alfred and Bruce Wayne are standing in the Batcave trying to get inside the Joker's head and understand his motives. They just can't figure out what he wants. Then Alfred decides to tell a long-winded story from back when he was in Burma. In Burma, Alfred explains, there were some bandits that stole valuable gems from the local government, and Alfred went looking for these bandits. He searched the forests for six months, but he didn't find anyone that the bandit had done business with. After all these months, one day, Alfred found a child holding a gem the size of a small fruit. The bandit had just been throwing the gems away. Bruce is shocked. He asks Alfred why would the bandit do that? Alfred takes a pause and then he says, "some men aren't looking for anything logical like money," and then Alfred concludes in dramatic style, "some men just want to watch the world burn."

As the theoretical reasons for why various types of dynamic pricing work are laid out, one thing becomes abundantly clear. The baseline assumption that serves as the foundation for all those theoretical reasons, is that people are economically rational. This is not a fully bad assumption. A lot of times people do things for rational economic reasons. Yet, the assumption isn't perfect.

When my maternal Grandfather came to visit the United States a few years ago, it was notable to me how little money he was choosing to spend. One of the key backers of a mall back home, you would expect him to partake in consumerism. Instead, we would go out to stores, and he would see things he would like and then put them back. I know that this isn't a broader behavior, he isn't cheap, he usually spends money in exorbitant amounts. What exactly was going on?

The phenomenon didn't really crystalize for me until I had a conversation with a good friend of mine named Rodrigo. Rodrigo is from Brazil. We met at Georgetown University in Washington D.C. and while D.C. is known for being an expensive city, Rodrigo would often complain about mundane things being very expensive. Why?

It turns out, every time Rodrigo bought a bottle of water, he was converting the price from dollars into Brazilian Real. For us it was just a dollar, we couldn't use that to get anything else. But for him, it was four Real, and he could use that to get far more in Brazil.

Rodrigo explaining that to me opened my eyes to a far broader phenomenon, the same one that afflicted my grandfather but also afflicts each of us. We often weigh costs in comparative terms. In other words, something might feel really expensive because a similar good is cheaper elsewhere, or something might feel expensive because the nominal value is quite high compared to normal purchases, such as a car. But our mind constantly uses a series of heuristics to determine what is expensive and what isn't. Too often, this is done in arbitrary ways, hijacking our ability to be happy about what are, in fact, economically sound purchases.

Strictly speaking, there are at least two main issues with the assumption of economic rationality. Primarily, there are powerful non-economic reasons people make decisions. These reasons are based on identity and ideology. In other words, these purchases are driven by questions of how a product makes someone feel or see himself. For example, a flashy car may make someone feel young or accomplished. In order to interact with consumers on this level, companies need to understand and build brands. Secondarily, even when people make decisions for standard economic reasons, they don't do so perfectly. They can wrongly approximate the functional benefits of an item or incorrectly internalize the cost. As the example with Rodrigo and my Grandfather illustrates. Because of this, Scott Case, the former-CTO of Priceline clarifies, "I think one of the real issues is how do these pricing models deal with the psychology of the customer and their behavior and their mindset."

Georgetown is a premier area within DC. If you ever go shopping there, you'll notice brand after brand lined up on the street. Zara, Brooks Brothers, Ralph Lauren, there is simply no end to the examples of corporations that have built brands associated with their products on the main streets of Georgetown. Yet, what exactly is a brand? I can't buy it, or touch it, or even really see it. And how exactly does pricing interact with a brand?

A brand is something, that while intangible, is a verifiable asset. The brand of a company is simply the story that we associate with that company. Further, a brand is the story we associate with that company's products. For example, when we think of Apple we think of revolutionary innovation. When we think of Disney, we think of creativity and a certain childish happiness. Every company has a brand. Some are clear and powerful. Some of these stories motivate us to associate with a company. For example, an idealistic student who has hopes of changing the world often buys a Mac. Other brands are ill-defined, such as many corner shops, with little to no external messaging. Brands interact with our sense of identity is hard to quantify ways. They motivate us beyond simple calculations of cost and benefit.

How then does pricing enter the equation? Prices tell a story about a product, and therefore they tell a story about the company. The price of an item, what you have to give up to get it, will invariably affect your evaluation of that item, and that evaluation takes hold in a story. For example, we find Walmart to be family-friendly because of its low prices. Comparatively, we find an Audi A8 to be exclusive and desirable, in part, because of its hefty price tag. This is not to say, anyone who decides to sell an expensive car, no matter what the quality, will be able to achieve that brand. In fact, pricing must go hand in hand with other marketing strategies like advertising. However, it is a tangible tool in the brand building toolbox. As Kyle Thompson-Westra, a pricing consultant at Wiglaf pricing, explains, "pricing is definitely tied up in branding." He furthers, "something like Black Friday or Cyber Monday is a good example." How then can prices be used to effectively build brands?

One specific example of this phenomenon is something almost every Georgetown student is familiar with. Wingo's Wednesday is a weekly discount of 50 percent off chicken wings on Wednesdays. Wingo's is a wings restaurant whose main clientele is college students. Every Wednesday, college students will line up around the block to buy wings for half-off. Why exactly is this story being told? Wingo's wants to appeal to students, who are invariably on budgets. The brand Wingo's is trying to build is one of affordable food. By having this habitual event, that idea is being hammered into students' heads over and over again. In fact, in a student's belief that they are saving tons of money, Wingo's often finds that students buy other items at the restaurant while there. This ends up bringing that customer's total spending above the amount they would have otherwise spent.

Does Wingo's make money on Wednesdays? No. As Mike Arthur, the owner of Wingo's, explains, everyone thinks he makes money because of the massive lines, but he loses money on the promotion. The drop-in margin is just too high. Further, the more sales he makes at these lower prices, the more his company hurts due to the negative margin on each unit. However, in his calculation, the associated brand-building that goes with the discount is worth the loss of revenue. As he says, "You got to do it." In his view, Wingo's Wednesday serves as an advertisement for Wingo's, helping to boost business on other days.

As prices increasingly go dynamic, then, how will this change branding? Should companies attempting to build brands not go dynamic? At this stage in the adoption of dynamic pricing where many markets are rapidly approaching a critical mass but dynamic pricing is still in early stages, there are still a lot of questions with no definitive answers. Some make the argument that if the role of price in branding is to help tell a story about a product, then by dynamically changing the price, the story itself constantly shifts. As such, a lack of consistency prevents a brand from being built. As Thompson-Westra corroborates, "Brands with a certain amount of cachet are just not going to discount their products." For example, dynamic pricing where the price of a Gucci belt could go down would hurt Gucci's overall branding. In the opposite market, you might argue that Wingo's Wednesday wouldn't be the same unless they could advertise half-off. So what is the outlook for dynamic pricing? Is it truly incompatible with overall branding pushes?

Firstly, there are ways brands can be built around dynamic pricing. For example, Uber tells the story of a company obsessed with efficiency through its dynamic pricing. We come to trust Uber as more reliable, and its pricing strategy helps build that brand.

Secondly, there is nothing inherent to dynamic pricing that disallows brand building. Instead, dynamic pricing can be tweaked. For example, Wingo's Wednesday would be not significantly different if the price were allowed to oscillate between a floor of a 30-percent discount and a ceiling of 50-percent discount depending on how busy the store was. Probably neither of those discounted prices is the correct market clearing price, but in the interests of branding, dynamic pricing can be used to create the perception of affordability while minimizing losses, even if they must occur. The concerns that this would dilute the message are overblown. The general concept is still in place: Even if the price slightly varies, it is still consistent with that message.

Lastly, dynamic pricing can be used to create other market conditions that also can help create a brand. What do I mean? There is a store called Georgetown Cupcake where people will wait in line without fail for at least 15 minutes to get a cupcake. Georgetown Cupcake sets their prices artificially lower than they could get away with so that people will wait in line in this way. In their view, that line serves as a message to other consumers that those cupcakes are worth waiting for, that they are an object that should be desired. Now imagine if they could use dynamic pricing to guarantee that there would always be a 20-minute wait. For example, instead of using dynamic pricing algorithms built around revenue or profit maximization, one could be used that maximizes customer volume. In this way, they would always be sure that their brand was being protected. Or if another store wanted to achieve similar status, they could use this tactic temporarily to get the ball rolling.

Ultimately, the revolution around pricing means that there are tremendous opportunities opening up around welding together dynamic pricing and branding, to create a dynamic branding. Those who can effectively do both will end up dominating markets because of the way that combination turbocharges their competitive advantage.

Yet even if questions of branding were taken out of the equation, there are still questions about how well people respond to changes in price. Does the difference between 10 percent off and 12 percent off meaningfully change motivations? It does in our economic models, but what about in real life? A TV show of all things, explains how this isn't necessarily a flaw precluding the efficacy of dynamic pricing, but rather can actively become a feature of it.

There are many startlingly incisive scenes on Mad Men, a drama set in 1960s New York, a world of corporate advertising, consumerism, and cocktails. Yet, one stands out above the rest. Roger Sterling, a partner of the advertising firm bearing his name, asserts, "I'll tell you what brilliance in advertising is: 99 cents. Somebody thought of that." (Bianchi). In saying that, Roger is able to peer into the average consumer's soul to extract an invaluable insight with surgical precision.

Dynamic pricing models and all pricing models, often take consumer rationality as a given assumption. And people are rational, but as Roger implicitly points out, they are rational only to a point. There is a very marginal difference between $1.00 and $0.99, but that simple price change works to skyrocket sales.

Why does this work? Simply because humans are not machines. We can't do multivariable calculus in our heads to always make the "economically" correct purchase. Instead, people have cognitive biases. These cognitive shortcuts help us make sense of a world overloaded with sensory inputs. Our cognitive flaws are many. For example, we overweight and underweight probabilities, we have hindsight bias, and we answer questions differently depending on how they are framed. These are just the tip of the iceberg.

Some of our cognitive biases affect how we perceive prices. There are a lot of different hypotheses for why $0.99 is perceived as disproportionately cheaper than $1.00. Professor Schindler of Rutgers University observes that consumers "perceive a 9-ending price as a round-number price with a small amount given back." Another explanation is that humans overweight the figures on the left side of the decimal in our evaluation of how costly an item is. Because of this, $0.99 feels much cheaper than $1.00, just like $5.99 feels much cheaper than $6.00.

There is a whole field of study devoted to how irrational biases affect price perception called psychological pricing. Going forward, dynamic pricing will therefore have to reconcile traditional economic models with these more nuanced behavioral models. For example, a computer algorithm based on traditional economic models could spit out $19.03 as the market-clearing price of a baseball ticket, but if that ticket was priced at $18.99, a person would be far more likely to buy it. A small four-cent reduction in margin could increase sale volume massively.

Dynamic pricing and psychological pricing are not incompatible. In fact, it is not only likely but actively inevitable that behavioral models integrate with traditional economic models when dynamic pricing decisions are made. In the example above, the change would be as simple as rounding the price down by 4 cents. While different cognitive biases might require more nuanced changes, these changes can be built into the computer algorithms, and in fact, they will. This is because eventually one dynamic pricing consulting company will do this, and all companies will be forced to either adapt or die. Such are the realities of the free market.

PART 2

DYNAMIC PRICING MODELS

CHAPTER 7

WHEN IS DYNAMIC PRICING BEST?

———

Finding the right pricing strategy can be a lot like finding a date on Tinder. You can use some filtering criteria to swipe left and eliminate clearly unsuitable partners. In this mental model, maybe one pricing strategy is too tall or another is too short. Maybe one lives too far away. You can swipe left for all of those. However, you can also swipe right to try those pricing strategies that meet your initial criteria. From there, if the date doesn't work out, you can go right back to Tinder. If it does work out, you and your pricing strategy could be raising children soon!

Well, what exactly are those make-or-break criteria? How can one know if dynamic pricing is right for his or her business?

Although there are many different types of dynamic pricing—each differently suited to a different market—economically speaking, high sale volume, fluctuating demand and perishable goods are all generally important indicators of how suitable dynamic pricing is for your industry. If you have all three characteristics, then you should feel out the problem of backlash before choosing whether or not to move further.

Primarily, sale volume is a key prerequisite. The whole logic behind dynamic pricing is that if you lower your prices, you'll sell more units, enough to make up for the loss of margin. However, if you're in a business where sale volume is limited regardless of price, then you won't sell that much more, and you'll end up losing money if you lower your prices. The same logic is also true for raising prices. In markets with low sale volume, it is better to optimize a singular price as opposed to investing in logistics around changing prices. An example of that type of industry would be private jet companies. They sell a few jets a month. Dynamic pricing for them would not make much sense. Food, retail, tickets, transportation—these are all industries with high sale volume, and these are the industries where dynamic pricing can thrive best.

Secondarily, large demand fluctuation is key for really effective dynamic pricing. This point is best illustrated through a thought experiment. Imagine your price was free-floating. In other words, it adjusted magically according to supply and demand. Now imagine five people walk into your store every 20 minutes. No matter what time of day it is, the number of people who want to buy your good is the same. In other words, imagine constant demand. Now since the price is free-floating, under those conditions, the price will be exactly the same at all times because demand does not change. In other words, unless demand fluctuates, it is structurally impossible to be both revenue-maximizing and dynamically pricing.

Thirdly, perishable goods make dynamic pricing actively necessary. Spoilage means that if you don't sell something in your inventory, you lose the entire value of that good because it goes bad. Now if you are in a perishable goods market like the restaurant industry, you would rather sell something at a 50 percent loss rather than a 100 percent loss. This means that through dynamic pricing, such as lowering prices before some of your inventory starts to spoil, you can increase revenue substantially and avoid total losses. Many businesses with high fixed costs but low variable costs also suffer from this problem. One example is a barbershop where employees sit around all day because no one comes in. The spoilage here is time. Unable to cut hair, the barber is losing out on his ability to produce economic output. If the barber offered a discount, he might not get the same profit margin he is used to, but it would still be higher than no margin whatsoever. Other examples of this same phenomenon include spas, nail salons, and other personal grooming services, generally.

So, let's say you meet all these criteria. How can you know if you should try dynamic pricing? Just like how you would go on a date with a person you met on Tinder, you need to metaphorically "go on a date" with dynamic pricing strategies before you can decide if you want to pursue a more serious relationship. There are a few ways to do this.

Firstly, you can look to other businesses in your industry that have adopted dynamic pricing. Did they have backlash? If so, how much? Is there a way to avoid what they went through? Secondly, you can dip your toe in the water by trying out dynamic pricing on a limited basis, in the same way that the San Francisco Giants did. Many dynamic pricing platforms offer free trials. Lastly, if everything continues to go your way, you can announce your intention to go fully dynamic to your consumers in a public way. If the backlash is still minimal, you ought to move forward to the final step: You should weigh the expected cost, in terms of adapting to dynamic pricing and the backlash risk, against the expected reward—profit and revenue increases potentially in the double digits. If you think there is enough to be gained and not a lot at risk, then by all means, go forward.

While I would encourage any business to be bold and brave in exploring dynamic pricing options, I would never ask them to be blind to the potential risks, especially from a public relations standpoint. One company that has been thoroughly examined throughout this book has been Uber. Yet, Uber can teach us when not to implement dynamic pricing as much as it can teach us about when to implement it.

Uber operates in two markets. One is the consumer market, where it sets the price and matches consumers to drivers. For the overall service, this is the demand side. The second is the driver market, where Uber finds drivers, connects them to consumers and takes a cut of the fare. For the overall service, this is the supply side.

Uber and other ride-sharing services have pioneered how to match supply to demand through advanced algorithms and predictive modeling of what demand will look like within specific geographical areas. They dynamically price in the consumer market, and they have come under fire for doing so. Many consumers considered surge multiples price gouging. Partially because of this, Uber no longer shows customers a multiplier, showing customers a dollar-denominated surge fare instead. Still, the concept behind surge pricing is unchanged. Many people's unhappiness is largely unchanged as well.

Uber has always defended its use of dynamic pricing by explaining the economic fundamentals underpinning it. In fact, former Chief Executive Travis Kalanick responded to price gouging concerns when he wrote in an email, "We regularly do surge pricing when demand outstrips supply.

Remember, we do not own cars nor do we employ drivers. Higher prices are required in order to get cars on the road and keep them on the road during the busiest times. This maximizes the number of trips and minimizes the number of people stranded. The drivers have other options as well. In short, without Surge Pricing, there would be no car available at all." (Lowrey). This is clearly a full-throated defense of dynamic pricing. Yet what do Uber's actions tell us? How does Uber price its own take out of every fare? It turns out that Uber doesn't dynamically price in its driver market. In other words, it charges a fixed percentage fee that is constant, instead of the percentage fee going up and down to maximize revenue. Doesn't that seem a bit hypocritical?

It is important to note that if the price being set is dynamically derived, then any percentage of that is also dynamic in some sense. Yet the larger point still stands. While Kalanick was going on the record with his defense, it just so happened that Uber was charging a flat 20 percent cut from each fare, in addition to a booking fee. In other words, the price Uber charged its drivers was not fully dynamically determined. This internal inconsistency made very little sense. As The Economist confirms, "the inflexibility of Uber's matchmaking fee, a fixed 20% of the fare, means that it may fail to optimize the matching of demand and supply. In quiet times, when fares are low, it may work well. Suppose it links lots of potential passengers willing to pay $20 for a journey with drivers happy to travel for $15. A 20% ($4) fee leaves both sides content. But now imagine a Friday night, with punters willing to pay $100 for a ride, and drivers happy to take $90: there should be scope for a deal, but Uber's $20 fee means such journeys won't happen." ("Pricing the Surge"). Because Uber chose not to dynamically price its percentage cut of the fare, it seems as though it was leaving money on the table, if you believe the Travis Kalanick's arguments.

Eventually, Uber tried dynamically pricing its own cut. In 2015, as Ellen Huet reported, Uber experimented with "taking less commission—Uber down to 5%, and Lyft down to zero—at times when they wanted to lower rider fares but keep paying drivers so they wouldn't quit." However, Uber eventually reversed course, going back to its flat fee model. Why?

Firstly, switching the dynamic pricing in this market would probably have limited benefits. For example, imagine you were an Uber driver who had committed to driving for an entire Saturday because you needed the extra money to pay for health insurance. Uber has a lot of market power in this situation. It's not like you're going to go home—you need the revenue. In this case, Uber could just be exercising its monopoly power. You would work whether Uber was charging 25 percent or 15 percent once you had already committed to it. So why would Uber lower its take when your supply curve is so inelastic? Whereas surge pricing might make a big enough difference to drivers on Uber to actually change their behavior, small changes in the percentage cut would seemingly have a small impact on driver behavior. Applying this logic to the example of the punter who will pay $100 and the driver who will only accept $90, Uber seems to have found that the driver will be willing to accept $80 in a lot of cases. On a more macro scale, it may be the case that Uber could benefit a bit economically from switching to dynamic pricing, but the reward would be limited because many drivers have inelastic supply curves.

Secondly, the risk Uber would take for a limited reward could be quite large. Uber wants to avoid backlash from its drivers. If Uber dynamically priced and increased its cut of the fare after a few rides of a lower cut, drivers might become upset with the arbitrary nature of the cut being taken. Firstly, the complication of a changing percent in addition to the actual price of the ride changing dynamically could confuse drivers. Secondly, even if drivers could understand both the logistics and the economic arguments in favor of dynamic pricing in the long run, short-term uproar may be costly enough to prevent Uber from wanting to take the leap. If drivers are upset in a meaningful enough way, they may choose to leave for emotional reasons, despite all the economic incentives meant to keep them locked in.

Isn't this backlash risk also true of consumers? Yes, it is in many ways. But while consumers might complain, losing one consumer is not that harmful to Uber's overall health in the grand scheme. However, losing a driver has a far bigger impact because there are simply far fewer drivers than there are consumers. If you don't have enough drivers, wait times will go up, and more consumers will leave. While this can also work in reverse if large numbers of consumers leave, Uber probably anticipates that consumers can understand nominal price changes more than drivers can understand changes in both the percentage cut and the nominal price. Therefore, Uber might simply be more risk-averse with drivers.

What lesson can we learn from Uber's asymmetry in pricing strategy? We can initially conclude that Uber is making a mistake. Or, we can learn that even the best ideas are doomed to fail without public support. Sometimes, different markets require different pricing strategies. We can learn that sometimes it is hard to thread the needle. Increasing profits while also preventing backlash is a delicate dance that needs to be well-managed. Further, we can learn that even when dynamically pricing, it is fundamentally important to keep things simple. People can be convinced of things when they can understand them. If the formula becomes too complicated, it cannot be justified. If it cannot be justified, some backlash is inevitable.

Uber is in a competitive market where dynamic pricing makes the most sense. This is the larger consumer market, where consumers have all sorts of options for transportation. Uber is also in a market where it has a lot of market power—this is the driver market, where drivers often need Uber for extra revenue and are not responsive to small changes in how much they make. In this market, Uber has made the calculation that the risk of dynamic pricing backfiring through backlash is not worth the limited reward. As more and more ride-sharing companies proliferate and the market becomes more saturated, Uber might shift to a dynamic pricing strategy because drivers would have more options to switch to, increasing their supply elasticity. On the flip side, if Uber gained undisputed market share and turned into a total monopoly, they might start personalizing the cut they are taking based on individual drivers. They cannot do that right now because it would probably cause an uproar among drivers, who might then switch to other services or hurt the Uber brand in the media, preventing new drivers from joining. The most successful strategy depends on the dynamic of the market.

This example proves a salient point. Even Uber, a champion of dynamic pricing, concedes that dynamic pricing need not be the best option in every single market right now. While increasingly dynamic pricing will continue to proliferate into markets, there are some markets where other strategies might make more sense. In the status quo, Uber is in a limbo state, where fixed percentage fees actually might make the most sense for their driver market.

Yet for this one counterexample of how dynamic pricing isn't always right, there are magnitudes more examples of perishable goods industries in which dynamic pricing is right. In fact, those industries are rapidly undergoing all sorts of shifts in pricing in the status quo. Moreover, great opportunities lie beyond the horizon for anyone brave enough to try to build tools or content around how dynamic pricing is done.

CHAPTER 8

FIXED RULES DYNAMIC PRICING

———

Last summer, my friends and I were back home over the break, and many of my friends had internships in DC. To contextualize, in the eyes of college students internships are the worst. Nothing meaningful is ever learned. Moreover, tedious and menial busy work is not only tangential but actively central to the work that interns are assigned. Often, interns are not assigned any work at all. If you want to know what boredom and unsatisfaction look like, walk into the intern cubicles at any major corporate office.

Unsatisfied with the coffee runs they were forced to do at their internships, two of my friends, Arnav and Mark, got together and decided to use their free time at their respective offices in a more productive way. They split DC's neighborhoods among themselves and created a Google drive document. The purpose of the doc was simple. Both Arnav and Mark needed to find and codify happy hour deals at bars in their chosen neighborhoods for every day of the week. During work, they would use their desktops to research happy hour advertisements, instead of fully devoting themselves to proofing memos. After work, Arnav and Mark would often meet each other at their newest find, for a drink at a discount. They made a game out of the doc. Whoever found the cheapest happy hour would get a free drink from the other. Weirdly, over the course of the summer, Arnav kept finding the cheapest places, forcing Mark to buy him free drinks. One day, as Mark bought Arnav yet another drink, he complained, "I don't know how you've done it, but the law of large numbers has been temporarily suspended."

Months later Arnav told me, "I have another friend from my internship who already had access to a doc with all the happy hours compiled." In other words, some earlier generation of interns had already done the legwork. It was a great con. Arnav did not have to do any searching at all, every day he would just pull up that doc, and choose the best venue for the given day. Mark still doesn't know that he was swindled for an entire summer.

What does this story have to do with dynamic pricing? It highlights a particular form of dynamic pricing—fixed-rules dynamic pricing. Early bird menus, happy hours at bars, different prices for lunch and dinner menus are all examples of fixed-rules dynamic pricing done within the food and drink industry. These strategies date far before recent technological shifts. In these sorts of dynamic pricing strategies, the intuition that the restaurant will be busy during dinner is used as a proxy for an actual measurement of demand, leading to higher prices at dinner. Or as in the earlier example, lower prices at targeted times entice people like my friends Arnav and Mark, as well as an entire generation of young professionals, to go get a drink after work. While not perfect, these simple intuitions have allowed restaurants and bars to better revenues for many decades.

Overall, fixed-rules dynamic pricing is a great dynamic pricing solution in markets where either computational or technological power is limited or where consumers need a clear and simple sense of how prices are going to dynamically change. Additionally, this type of dynamic pricing is very cheap to implement because it doesn't require heavy technological integration or extensive economic modeling, both of which can be expensive in both effort and cost. Furthermore, because of its cost-effectiveness, it is a good intermediate step. This is particularly true if you want to run a natural experiment to see if changing prices is effective in your market, or if there is going to be a lot of backlash that will motivate consumers to shop elsewhere. Like dipping your toe in the water, running a trial with fixed-rules dynamic pricing doesn't require extensive integration with marketplaces, can be done cheaply, and can be done in a limited way to find out if there is a pricing strategy that can be better for you.

Dan Leahy, the former CEO of Savored, was really treading on a well-established trail when he founded Savored. As opposed to using computational techniques to do revenue-management dynamic pricing, Savored decided to use flat 30-percent discounts in order to keep things simple for consumers and businesses. These discounts were offered during off-peak hours of any restaurant's choosing. While high-end restaurants were empty before at certain times—such as from 2 p.m. to 5 p.m.—after joining Savored, the restaurants suddenly saw an influx of customers during that time, as customers would book meals on Savored.com. This was entirely due to the fixed-rule dynamic pricing scheme that was implemented. As Dan explained to me, the decision to choose fixed-rule as opposed to revenue-management was partly motivated by the need to protect the dignity of the restaurant so that they didn't have to negotiate for nickels and cents every time a customer walked in.

Yet there are too many markets where even this simple form

of dynamic pricing, one that doesn't require any major technology or computational ability, has not taken hold.

If you've ever been to a barber shop, you know the protocol. My father used to take me to get haircuts on Sundays. We would go to the barbershop near our house and sit in the waiting area, sometimes for over half an hour, as seemingly each of my neighbors got his or her hair cut before me. My dad seemed quite content to read the magazines, but as a child, I was thoroughly bored. The only thought in my head used to be "Why do we have to wait for soooo long?

Arik Levinson is a professor of economics at Georgetown University. As with any economist, Professor Levinson's mind is constantly analyzing the world through economic models. Once, while we were talking about both of our respective experiences at the barber shop, Professor Levinson told me a story about a time he went to his barber on a Saturday.

His barber would always be shockingly full on Saturdays and as shockingly empty on most other days. One day, Professor Levinson asked the barber a very simple question: "Why don't you just charge more on Saturdays?" When considered from a traditional economic model of rational decision-making, the economic grounds for raising prices on Saturdays were solid. Raising prices at a time when demand was higher would increase revenues for the barber and lower wait times for the customer. The barber thought Levinson's suggestion was quite odd. Here was a customer actively asking to have to pay more. Furthermore, the barber responded that raising prices wouldn't be fair. It seemed morally intuitive to the barber that he should charge one fixed price all the time—otherwise, different people would get different treatment.

Professor Levinson later thought a lot about his conversation with that barber. He wondered why he should expect the barber to have uniform pricing all the time if he couldn't expect a flight on Thanksgiving weekend to be the same price as one on a random weekday.

Slowly, large corporations are starting to pick up on Professor Levinson's line of reasoning—at least one large corporation, that is.

There is perhaps no company that has revolutionized entertainment from the 20th to 21st century as much as Disney. Disney has consistently been at the forefront of innovation, from synchronizing sound and picture to pioneering animated films. That long arc of innovation is now being realized in some of their pricing decisions: Disney has gone dynamic.

Growing up as part of the Pixar generation, *Toy Story* and *Toy Story 2* were my favorite movies. My mother had this running joke that if she had a dollar for every time I watched *Toy Story* on the DVD player, she would be a billionaire. I was truly a fanatic. In fact, I used to dress up as Buzz Lightyear almost every Halloween. When I was eight or nine, my parents finally took me to Disney World to actually meet the "real" Buzz Lightyear. We left right before Christmas.

I went in with tremendously high expectations. The second you walk through those gates, you're awed at the sight of all your heroes, whether they be the Power Rangers, Buzz Lightyear or Cinderella and Snow White. These are the characters whose stories live in your imagination. You spend all day playing with their action figures. At night, you sleep with those action figures by your side. Once you reach the park, you finally get to meet people dressed up as those characters. You can collect their autographs. You can even go on their rides and walk around the park. Despite all of this, my experience was one of both delight and disappointment.

As you might know, children very rarely get blocks of time off from school during the school year. Whenever they do, parents try to take advantage by going on vacation. This is why tourism spikes during winter break and spring break. In fact, this is never truer than in the weeks and days surrounding Christmas. There are certain destinations that this phenomenon particularly affects, and Disney World is one of them.

When I went to Disney World with my family during the week of Christmas, the theme park was absolutely packed. My parents tried to navigate through the overcrowding by waking us up earlier to get to the park earlier. However, no matter how early we got there, eventually the park would start to fill up throughout the day. For most of our time at the park, we were constantly wading through the crowd.

How did this impact us and every other family there? When there is that much overcrowding, everyone is immensely worse off. For example, the second you try to get on the ride that corresponds to your favorite character, you realize that the hourlong wait means you have to stand there in the blistering sun for 60 whole minutes—all this for a ride that will last a grand total of less than five. This is really bad for consumers like my family and me.

In my case specifically, on our last day at the park, I finally spotted Buzz Lightyear in the distance. I was ecstatic. I told my parents we had to go meet him, so we started to move in that direction. However, a lot of other young boys and girls had seen him too, because, by the time we got to Buzz Lightyear, he was surrounded by roughly 40 kids. I wanted an autograph more badly than anything, but in the chaos, he ignored me. My heart sank.

With the story framed this way, raising prices at times of

absurdly high demand seems to make a lot of sense for the consumer. For example, if prices went up and fewer people chose to go to Disney World, then each person left at Disney World would be far better off. If this had been true when I was eight years old, I wouldn't have had to wait an hour in line for each ride I wanted to go on. More importantly, Buzz Lightyear would have noticed me.

The case for dynamic pricing at Disney World is rather straightforward. If prices adjust with demand, then I no longer have to wait as much even when demand is very high because price rations entrance into Disney World so that fewer people can go. However, the price also goes down during off-peak seasons so that more people can go. Consumers are better off because the quality of their experience is guaranteed, and Disney is better off because they can increase revenue.

Thankfully, I've never been in charge of organizing family vacations. However, I can imagine that one day this responsibility will fall on me. If I decided to spend time planning out a vacation weeks in advance, then I would be incredibly upset if my scarce vacation time on a cruise or a beach did not go as planned. In fact, on any vacation, I value my time—which is limited to a week at most—more than my money. Applying this broadly to Disney World, when I pay hundreds of dollars to travel to, stay at and enjoy Disney World, I value my time in that park far way more than I value an additional dollar; the trade-off for me is quite clear. I would much rather pay a higher price for smaller crowds because I will not be able to go back to Disney World again anytime soon. Money is fungible—I can make it back. Time is a one-way street for me, and I won't be back at Disney World for a while.

Not everyone thinks like this. People who live near the park might be turned off by the higher price. People choosing between Disney World and Universal might choose Universal instead. People with the option to change their vacation dates might move their scheduled time at Disney World. However, those who value Disney World the highest during peak times— such as my family and me when I was eight—will choose to go to the park at a higher rate. This leaves Disney World with fewer overall people but more revenue from significantly higher-paying customers.

As for Disney, they've branded Disneyland as "the happiest place on Earth." For both of their parks in the United States and the many ones abroad, Disney needs to protect these sorts of branded images by maintaining the quality of the parks. Pricing is one way to do that. Further, increasing prices, at times of high demand, also maximizes revenue for Disney. This is why, as of 2016, Disney decided to increase prices by 20% at times of peak demand at Disney World and Disneyland. They implemented a simple fixed-rules dynamic pricing scheme, they've codified certain times of the year as peak demand times, and they've implemented higher prices around those times. This is fixed-rules dynamic pricing, as opposed to some other form of dynamic pricing, specifically because the price will go up by a set amount at a set time, just like a happy hour at a restaurant. With Disney tickets everything is announced ahead of time. As the Economist explains, "Prices will be higher at certain times of the year, but parents will not arrive at the gates of Animal Kingdom to find that a glimpse of the massive artificial tree has doubled in price since they left the house." ("Disney Discovers Peak Pricing").

Lastly, the increased revenues can be used to manage the excess demand in a better way. Disney can use the extra money to invest in increasing capacity for Disneyland and Disney World to in the longer term. It can solve back for some of the structural constraints that lead to the sort of lines because there are only a limited number of rides. When they are more rides than the carrying capacity of the park increases, which means in the future more people are able to go and enjoy the park at any time of year. At least in the short term, it makes a tremendous amount of sense to use dynamic pricing to smooth out the demand side.

Why use fixed-rules dynamic pricing instead of revenue management? After all, they are both responses to the same market conditions, but revenue management is simply a more precise way to actually fluctuate pricing? The answer is that illogical though it may sound, there are benefits in being less precise. Primarily, fixed-rules may be seen as more fair, because even though prices will still change, consumers know ahead of time how they will change. As such, it may be easier for consumers to understand why or how prices are changing and make decisions accordingly. As such this type of dynamic pricing may better convey an aura of fairness. As we already know, that can be important to consumers who decide what to purchase based on non-economic reasons.

The predictability of fixed-rules dynamic pricing, however, is also a double-edged sword. While predictability is perceived as more fair, it can also be abused by consumers. In fact, if employed for long periods of time in a predictable way, fixed-rules dynamic pricing can lead to cannibalization. Cannibalization is when customers who would have otherwise paid full price start only buying at cheaper prices. If you broadcast that prices will be lower from time A to time B, then many consumers can just wait it out and choose *only* to buy at the times when prices are cheaper.

Cannibalization affects different businesses differently. Therefore, it is each business' responsibility to gauge the magnitude of the cannibalization problem. A very simple test is to see if a happy hour, for example, is increasing business at slow times while keeping other times relatively constant or if its increasing business at slow times at the expense of other times.

Often times cannibalization will be small, and therefore fixed-rules dynamic pricing will still be a net positive. If cannibalization has a largely negative impact, that doesn't necessarily mean that dynamic pricing is wrong for you. Instead, it can mean that revenue management might be a better option because, as you'll learn in the next chapter, revenue management algorithms adjust to cannibalization practices and prevent losses.

From a theoretical economic perspective, fixed-rules dynamic pricing is better in perishable goods markets than fixed prices, but it is not as efficient as other forms of dynamic pricing such as revenue management. However, these theoretic economic models do not take into account risks like consumer backlash. Therefore, fixed-rules dynamic pricing can be best to maintain an aura of fairness because the rules are announced in advance, as in the case of Disney. Most importantly, fixed-rules dynamic pricing can be best as a way to try dynamic pricing techniques in a low-cost way to check for backlash before transitioning to revenue management dynamic pricing.

CHAPTER 9

REVENUE MANAGEMENT DYNAMIC PRICING

———

Priceline's bold idea was the "name your own price" tool. Whereas airlines had been doing revenue management dynamic pricing for decades before Priceline came along, Priceline fully inverted the script. Just like eBay helps you bid on items that you want, instead of letting the producer set a price, so too did Priceline allow consumers to bid for airline tickets and hotel rooms. For example, if I wanted an airplane ticket to Boston, I could go to Priceline, find a ticket, and say that I would be willing to pay $70 at the most for a ticket. The airline companies, utilizing Priceline, could then decide if it was in their best interests to sell me a ticket or wait for better offers given their current stock of tickets and the amount of demand for those tickets. As you can intuitively guess, when demand was higher or supply was lower, the prices accepted by the companies were much higher. On the other hand, when demand was lower and supply was higher, prices accepted by the companies were much lower. If there were a lot of seats left, which would otherwise go unfilled, many low bids were accepted because some revenue is better than no revenue. On the other hand, if the flight was packed, or nearly packed, on the day of the flight, only the highest bids could capture a seat.

The ruthless effectiveness of revenue management can be illustrated by Priceline's example. Priceline was first founded by Scott Case and Jay Walker as a demand collection tool. As Scott Case told me the framing around the business was built around a question. He posited that instead of doing revenue management from the supply side with producers setting prices in ways that might upset consumers, "why can't we flip that around and give the customer the opportunity to declare their demand and their willingness to pay a price and you can marry those two things up and in that way fill up airplane seat and hotel rooms." When Scott Case first approached airlines with this idea, they were extremely hesitant. They didn't want to have to give up their ability to control their own prices. Yet, as soon as Scott showed them the actual Priceline, the demand curve that they were able to draw after collecting all the individual bids for any given plane seat or hotel room, the opposition of airline companies started to melt.

The example of Priceline also best showcases the role that perishable goods have to play in revenue management pricing systems. A perishable good, is a good that expires or loses all value at a certain point in time. For example, a hotel room that goes unbooked and a plane seat that goes cross-country empty are both examples of perishable goods. The science of revenue management is able to use algorithms to determine, what sort of discounts to offer given the timeline available before a good expires. For example, sometimes it is profit-maximizing to take a loss when you sell a particular hotel room or plane seat if the alternative is making no money at all. Therefore, revenue-management dynamic pricing systems not only match prices with fluctuating demand but also keep careful inventory of diminishing supply.

This is particularly true in the restaurant industry. As I went around talking to restaurants while the team was building features for the Dynos app, one of the most popular motivations to join a platform like Dynos was the fact that so much food went to waste. My good friend Rodrigo used to work for an on-campus coffee shop at Georgetown University. Speaking about the sheer waste at the shop, he estimated that, "anywhere from an eighth to a sixth of the food goes to waste."

Through an algorithm that adjusts discount levels based on inventory and approximate levels of demand, Dynos is able to get in customers to eat that produce at a discount. By doing that we can save it from the terrible fate of being thrown away. Moreover, we can generate a substantial increase in revenue for the restaurant to boot.

Revenue management dynamic pricing is a response to the same economic factors that fixed-rules dynamic pricing attempts to respond to. Namely, these are as follows: demand that shifts markedly throughout time, low variable costs, high fixed costs, and often time perishable goods. The difference between fixed-rules dynamic pricing and revenue management is that revenue management is a more precise answer to the same problem. This is because whereas fixed-rules dynamic pricing attempts to approximate demand through some pattern of what demand is associated with, revenue management actually measures it. For example, a happy hour menu from 3 PM to 5 PM generally assumes that no one will be at the restaurant at those times absent an incentive. Contrastingly, Dynos measures and models how many consumers would be at a restaurant at a given time, instead of assuming it. Furthermore, Dynos optimizes the most beneficial discount in the case that the restaurant can make more revenue by lowering prices.

Revenue management requires more computational power than other forms of dynamic pricing. It also requires some way to broadcast information about price changes, because it does not matter how sophisticated your algorithm is if consumers don't know that your prices have changed. Increasingly, through marketplace apps and websites like Dynos, Priceline, or Uber, third-party companies are providing businesses or individuals with the required computational power and a medium to transmit information to consumers. Revenue management, therefore, is the form of dynamic pricing that has most been accelerated by the technological shifts that have made that sort of computation possible and accessible for broad swaths of people. If the market conditions described earlier apply to you, then revenue management dynamic pricing is the best way to proceed if you have access to computational tools and a way to disperse information, like a marketplace. It is also best if you are certain that you won't face much backlash or if you have already tried fixed-rules dynamic pricing and have not received any backlash. Often times, committing to revenue management requires some costs, such as training your employees to deal with Dynos deals, but these costs are well worth the substantial rewards to increased revenue throughout the day, and lower losses from spoilage of perishable goods.

Increasingly, if fixed-rules dynamic pricing is something that your business has successfully engaged in, then it makes complete sense to go all the way to revenue management because of its superior precision and decreasing costs. But while technological shifts and marketplace developments online and on apps have accelerated the use of revenue management, the airline industry has been doing it for decades by quoting different prices for tickets as the departure date nears, even before Priceline gave them the knowledge of exactly what people were willing to pay. But how exactly does revenue management pricing work so precisely?

There is no one better to explain how it works than someone whose daily wage depends on revenue-management dynamic pricing. So one day while I was taking an Uber around Washington, D.C., I just started asking my Uber driver, Sisay, about how he goes about his job as an Uber driver. I asked him, "Which areas do you usually target and why?" Sisay responded, "I drive rush hours in Georgetown and Morgan Adams and Northwestern part of D.C., and mostly that is surge."

In other words, through the use of monetary incentives like higher prices, Uber was able to position a driver like Sisay in the high-demand areas that needed him most. If you zoom out and realize the scope of Uber and other ridesharing companies' data, it becomes clear what the premise of revenue management is: using pricing to bring supply and demand into equilibrium at every moment. As Sisay explains, if he ever hits a dry streak where he consistently gets a series of low fares, "I turn off my app and go to hotel areas. There's a chance—it's not guaranteed—but there's a chance [of surge].

50-50." Eventually, as people just like Sisay flock to hotels, surge pricing ends there too. Then it's on to the next place, and the one after that. Uber keeps its pieces moving at breakneck speed, constantly maximizing revenues and lowering wait times with surgical precision.

If it wasn't already abundantly clear, the reason revenue management is superior to traditional fixed pricing is twofold. This recently clicked for me in a very tangible sense after I came back to Washington, D.C., from Penn Station. To contextualize, my friends and I had gone to New York for the weekend, and after a fantastic weekend, we were absolutely tired. So we slept on the train all the way back to Union Station. After the roughly four hours it took to get to D.C., we groggily got up and off the train. A few minutes later, we dragged our suitcases through the front door of Union Station and got to work looking for transportation back to Georgetown University.

At that moment, we half-tiredly pulled out our phones to find an Uber. We didn't even consider taking one of the many cabs that were right in front of us, parked and ready to go. This habitual, and subconscious, anchoring to ridesharing, illustrates just how pervasive marketplaces like Uber have become to my generation. Further, that specific moment revealed to me just how ingrained ridesharing has become as our default transportation choice.

As we looked down on our screens, there was surge pricing in effect because everyone from the train who just got off was doing the exact same thing. Still, the price was lower than what a taxi would have charged. We bit the extra cost and got in an Uber, making our way back home after a long night.

Arik Levinson, a professor of economics at Georgetown University, made the counterfactual decision. A few weeks earlier he had taken a flight back to Washington-Dulles Airport. As he exited the airport, he too checked his Uber app. However, surge pricing was in effect. A man from an earlier generation, Professor Levinson took a cab instead. What does this counterfactual tell us?

Reflecting back on his decision, Levinson said that this experience made him question why cabs still exist. There are two distinct scenarios. Firstly, if Uber is cheaper than a cab, then the cab will not get any revenue because consumers will choose to use Uber. This is what my friends and I did. Secondly, if the cab is cheaper than the Uber, it is because they are leaving revenue on the table because they have not optimized their prices. In other words, the cab company should have charged Professor Levinson more, and he would still have chosen the cab as long as it was still at least marginally lower than Uber. However, because the cab companies don't dynamically price in a lot of circumstances, they will continue to bleed out to ridesharing companies like Uber and Lyft, either through lost customers or insufficient revenue.

Moreover, revenue management solves the problem of cannibalization in a simplistic way. Cannibalization occurs when customers think they can get a better price later, so they stop buying at higher prices now. However, if revenue management algorithms are in place then if everyone starts trying to buy at lower prices later, those prices will instantly increase at those times. Interestingly on the flip side, if people stop buying at higher prices now, then the price will instantaneously drop now, creating incentives to consume now. The near constant adjustment of the market means that cannibalization cannot truly eat into your margins in the same way that cannibalization can in fixed-rules dynamic pricing. The precision solves the problem.

Despite its obvious profitability, public discussions involving revenue management have increasingly focused on the ethical dilemmas surrounding it. It is important to understand these critiques for two reasons. Firstly, if revenue management can result in unethical behavior there is a moral obligation for all of us to make changes to the practice. Secondly, these ethical debates can help inform how to avoid backlash, from a strategic business point of view. Consider the following thought experiment:

A hurricane has just left hundreds of thousands of people devastated, the entire community is bursting at the seams. The surrounding area looks like a fractured picture, a disjointed puzzle. In the aftermath of the storm, right when you need a transportation most, Uber charges 400% more. How does that make you feel?

Your car is flipped over in your front yard, and you'll pay anything for transportation to any place that is capable of providing shelter. But is this fair? Uber chooses *now* to raise prices? Is there a deeper moral responsibility that companies like Uber are failing to meet in times of disaster? Framed in this way, the story probably makes you angry with Uber. You see them as price gougers and parasites, but is there an underlying economic justification? Or are these exorbitant excesses of greedy corporations with too much market power? As it turns out, there might be an economic case to be made. Ex-Uber CEO Travis Kalanick certainly thinks so. Responding to surge pricing after a 2013 snowstorm, he said, "We did more trips because of our approach, not fewer." (Isaac).

In late 2013, New York City suffered from a massive snow storm. While not as dramatic as a hurricane, this emergency situation illustrated Uber's philosophy in these sorts of situations. Uber's argument is simple. It's an argument that free-market ideologues make all the time. We're focusing on the wrong side of the market.

While the conventional wisdom is to focus on the plight of people who've suffered from these massive tragedies, Uber says perhaps a forward-looking outlook, one that focuses on getting the most resources into the suffering area is the better mindset.

Post-hurricane, tsunami, flood, and snow storm, resources can be a matter of life and death sometimes. Prices that can dynamically adjust upwards do two things. Firstly, they force rationing. If a hotel is exorbitantly expensive you might share one with another family for a night. This means there's another room open for another two families and all of a sudden a building that would've held half the people the night before can hold double that capacity, as an entire community adjusts its resources. In the case of Uber, or taxis, or transportation more generally- this would mean squeezing as many people as possible into each car, instead of using two cars to fit the whole family. Secondly, higher prices increase incentives to bolster supply. If I'm an Uber Driver during an emergency situation, I will obviously be more likely to drive away to places where driving conditions are safer, if there is no countervailing incentive for my enduring the hardship of extreme weather. Yes, good Samaritans exist, but they exist regardless of whether or not surge pricing occurs. Suge pricing brings out those whose hearts are not quite as big. But if the price increases, all of a sudden all sorts of Uber drivers like me are attracted to the market. The supply of much-needed transportation arrives, and eventually, prices decrease again. As Kalanick said in the wake of the New York snowstorm, "we gave people more options to get around, and that is the whole frickin' goal." (Isaac).

Yes, it feels wrong that in time of disaster, people have to lose so much, but it's not just the fault of these companies. It's the fault of underlying factors. It's the fault of the hurricane. If the price doesn't go up, then suppliers aren't going to be incentivized to pump in the sort of resources. And yes it sounds cruel that people won't do it in time of need. But ultimately, that's how self-interested people make decisions in a lot of cases. This is what Uber and many businesses on the ground think.

Skeptics ask, "In times of need, are these corporations taking advantage of monopoly power when their competitors are shut down and unable to operate? Or are they just adjusting to the market as it is?" Perhaps self-interestedly, Kalanick asserts, "We are not setting the price. The market is setting the price." But is it? If it is the case that they're taking advantage of monopoly power to charge beyond the efficient price to make a maximal profit—as opposed to promoting public welfare—then maybe they are price gougers. Maybe they are parasites. But if, on the other hand, they're simply adjusting to the realities of the market try to help people, then maybe we need not be as concerned about price fluctuations.

This is still an open question, and dynamic pricing becomes more pervasive in other industries every day. Soon, emergencies or even times of mild difficulty—like minor car accidents—are going to be prone to instantaneous price fluctuations across a lot of different goods, like needed supplies. It's time we confront these types of economic and moral dilemmas now.

Ethics aside, revenue management dynamic pricing is rapidly proliferating through various marketplaces and tools. When you hear the phrase dynamic pricing, or see it on the cover of a book, you immediately think of this sort of dynamic pricing. This is what has largely captured the public's attention in the recent discourse around this issue.

Even in this book, we've already discussed revenue management in various contexts. For example, the San Francisco Giants used a form of revenue management when they dynamically priced their stadium tickets. Look at how that turned out for them. Not only did they prosper, but now almost the entirety of Major League Baseball does too. From all of these examples, it should be clear that revenue management dynamic pricing, especially in perishable goods markets, is very profitable- backlash aside. However, it should also clear that there needs to be either self-regulation on the parts of corporations or externally imposed regulation to make sure that in exigent circumstances, dynamic pricing does not become a tool to exploit the weak.

CHAPTER 10

CONDITIONAL RULES DYNAMIC PRICING

———

Conditional rules dynamic pricing differs from fixed-rules dynamic pricing in that intervening events, certain conditions, need to be met for prices to change. This sort of dynamic pricing is particularly useful as a tool to incentivize certain kinds of behaviors. For example, a conditional rule at a restaurant such as if there are fewer than ten customers sitting in at any given time, there is a 5% discount, would be an effective way to increase customers at slow times. Moreover, Conditional rules dynamic pricing is also particularly effective as a tool for businesses involved in intense competition with others, as the story of Wingo's illustrates.

Wingo's is a beloved institution. The broader Georgetown community has been going there for decades, and students at Georgetown University are positively enamored with the place. Today, Wingo's is the go-to stop for any student that craves chicken wings late at night or wants chicken wings delivered during the day. Yet, for a brief period of time at the turn of this decade, there was an intense winner-takes-all competition for the Georgetown chicken wing eating population.

Georgetown Wing Co. opened up right next to the campus in 2010. Wingo's, which had been in the neighborhood since 1983, finally had competition for the same customers in the exact same niche. While you might think being open for more than two decades longer would provide Wingo's with a massive incumbent advantage, two structural factors mitigated this. Firstly, every four years, students cycle out of the university. So for a senior at Georgetown, it had been as though Wingo's had only been there for four years. For a freshman, both companies were brand new. Because of this, brand loyalty and habitual buying habits were mitigated. Secondly, college students are notoriously fickle. Having a very high sensitivity to price changes, college students were fair game for both restaurants. The stage was set for a knife fight. Anything could happen.

Added to the inherently competitive dynamic of the market, was a personal dimension. Mike Arthur, the owner of Wingo's, is a friendly and fiercely loyal person. If he is ever forced to choose between making a customer happy or making more money, he almost always chooses to make the customer happy. However, he is still a businessman, and like any businessman, he is prideful. He's rightfully proud that he's built an operation that is able to succeed in a market where restaurants close and open with surprising frequency. He's proud of the brand he's built. As with anyone successful, there's a certain ego involved, where personal worth becomes intertwined with the product itself. His pride is not best described as hubris, but rather a sort of expectation of respect. On the flip side, the owner of Georgetown Wing Co was an ambitious young guy. He had an idea and went to his father for funding. His father set him up with a premier piece of real estate on M Street, Georgetown's main corridor. Again, there is an ego involved. Anyone who has started a business would be lying if they said that their sense of self-confidence didn't in at least some sense motivate their decision to become an entrepreneur. The owner of Georgetown Wing Co was no different. Determined and ambitious, he truly believed he could become an institution ingrained in the community the same way Wingos was.

Once Georgetown Wing Co. opened up, the Georgetown University student newspaper decided to do a wings competition between the two restaurants. The competition included a panel of judges who tried wings from both places. Both sets of owners were present at the competition. After an arduous and long tasting process, Wingo's eventually won. After the competition ended, the owner of Georgetown Wing Co. came up to Mike Arthur and said, "I might not have won this, but I'm going to be your biggest competition."

Reflecting back on that moment, Mike Arthur said about the owner of Georgetown Wing Co., "This kid was so arrogant, the young kid." He furthered, "I thought it was really adversarial." Not one to take a blow standing down, Mike Arthur responded, "Just to let you know, I've been here for a lot longer. My rent's nothing, I own the building. I can sell this food for free, I can give this food away for free while you choke and die on that rent." If the first comment was a cruise missile, Mike Arthur responded with a nuclear bomb. After saying that, he paused. A few seconds later, he repeated, "I can give it away for free. I can give it away." He paused again before asking, "How long can you do it for?" The owner of Georgetown Wing Co. was shell-shocked. He went home with his tail between his legs. The foreshadowing ended, and the real market competition began.

As Mike Arthur clarified, Georgetown Wing Co. had a $19,000 monthly rent. Due to the competitive advantage of the lack of rent in combination with superior quality, Wingo's eventually won the wings battle over the course of two years. Georgetown Wing Co. shuttered its doors. It was annihilated. Having arrived at Georgetown long after Georgetown

Wing Co. shut its doors, to me it was like it had never even existed. Describing his winning strategy, Mike Arthur said what he did was akin to how "the Chinese will dump on the market and drive out the competition."

What does this story teach us? How does this relate to dynamic pricing? Firstly, consider when Mike Arthur said, "I can give it away for free." This isn't what he did in real life, but it is illustrative to consider this counterfactual. Would that be the best strategy?

Presumably not. Taking no margins would guarantee a substantial marginal loss on each and every item Wingo's sold. While this might drive a competitor out of the market, any strategy is only as good as its inferior alternatives. In this case, the alternatives are substantially better.

One alternative is a form of dynamic pricing called conditional rules-based pricing. One example of this type of dynamic pricing would be pegging prices. This would have hammered Georgetown Wing Co. without costing Wingo's as much. Anytime Georgetown Wing Co. decreased its prices, Wingo's would decrease its prices, and then go slightly lower. To the marginal college student interested in buying wings then, Wingo's would always be the more attractive option. We see this sort of dynamic pricing in all sorts of online marketplaces. For example, retailers on Amazon will often change their prices multiple times a day depending on how their competitors are changing prices throughout the day.

In reality, Mike Arthur did a form of this type of pricing, but it wasn't as codified and there was some lag time. This is to be expected. The reason retailers can change their prices multiple times a day on Amazon is that all prices on Amazon are readily available electronically. This isn't always the case in traditional physical stores, although increasingly menus are going online through platforms like Grubhub, UberEats, and the app I've launched Dynos.

This story illustrates an important point. Pricing is often about more than just the fundamentals of your own business, it is about the competitive dynamics of all businesses in the marketplace. Many dynamic pricing strategies can account for that. Increasingly as physical stores go online, joining marketplaces, or launching their own websites, dynamic pricing that pegs their prices to their competitors' can help them win a larger war in these sorts of winner-takes-all markets.

Here's the crucial thing about dynamic pricing: It's dynamic. This is even more true for conditional rules-based dynamic pricing. You can apply it to different situations to maximize the effect it has on the economy. What's more, sometimes you can leverage it as an effective tool in order to leave not only one market better off, but multiple interconnected markets as well. This is especially true when the actor is the Government. Lest we forget, taxes are a price we pay. We pay that price for education, and transportation, and welfare. Often, taxes can even affect the prices of other goods too. Therefore, public policy can use dynamic pricing, of taxation, as a tool, in its toolbox, to correct market inefficiencies. In fact, we're increasingly seeing this happen.

The election of Mayor of London in 2000 featured political backstabbing that was every bit as dramatic as the Ides of March. But, lost in the fog of politics, was a policy proposal that was central to the race. This proposal, a congestion levy, was an innovative attempt at dynamic pricing by the government. Once implemented, Mayor Ken Livingston's congestion levy changed London forever.

By the dawn of this millennium, London had a terrible traffic problem. It was one of the worst in Europe. Everyone agreed that something had to be done. So in 2000, Ken Livingston ran on a platform that included introducing a congestion charge in the city center. Once implemented, the charge would increase the price of driving in the city center at certain times via a levy. Livingston was ostracized widely in the press. The London Evening Standard boldly proclaimed that he was "determined to destroy London." (Beckett). However, he won the election and implemented the policy, and the amount of normal traffic in the heart of the capital decreased by around 15 percent. (Morris).

What exactly was this congestion charge? Before the policy, the price, the tax citizens paid to use the roads in central London, was zero. This changed. The congestion charge was dynamic. The price was now either zero or a fixed amount, depending on whether it was an off-peak hour or a peak hour. Therefore, the price of driving on the road changed dynamically by the time of day and the location of your driving, with the charge only applying to the city center. When this idea was floated by Livingston's campaign, Steve Norris, Livingston's rival during the 2000 election said, "Livingstone's transport plans are in a shambles." (Beckett).

Yet to evaluate Mr. Norris' claim, we need to first understand why traffic happens. Simply put, it occurs because as decision-makers, we don't internalize what we're costing other people when we use the road. We selfishly and simply think that we've already paid for roads through our income taxes, and so we ought to be able to use them as we wish. However, there is a broader cost that we impose. When I drive at 6 p.m., I'm hurting everyone else on the road by contributing to traffic. This applies to each and every person on the road. Ultimately, traffic leaves everyone worse off because when the streets are flooded, no one can get where they're going. Not only is the infrastructure being wasted, but so is everyone's time.

Why did the congestion levy work? Prices change people's decision-making calculus. Instead of the marginal cost being zero for using the roads during busy times, it was now tens of pounds. Ever self-interested, people shifted from driving themselves to alternatives like taxis, carpooling, public transport and biking. Once the policy was implemented, these consumption shifts happened every day dynamically as the levy went into effect during certain hours. The citizens of London adjusted through various alternatives. As a result, London had a more efficient allocation of resources. Further, the decrease in the number of cars just waiting around due to traffic benefited whoever was left on the road. Finally, the roads were actually usable.

How did Livingston's government avoid the kind of backlash that has so often plagued dynamic pricing in the private sector? This is not an easy issue. Anytime prices increase dynamically, there will be people who are upset. After all, electoral politics is even more susceptible to a public backlash that can potentially lead to representatives being voted out, and their policies being repealed. In fact, this was a concern. In the lead up to the implementation of the policy, a spokesman for a transportation interest group proudly proclaimed,

"Livingstone's got a lot of courage." (Beckett). Yet, any backlash was mitigated because the public understood that something had to be done about the traffic. In their view traffic was a bigger tax than the actual tax.

Thus, a massive backlash never materialized. Instead, implementing the Congestion Charge allowed the City of London to increase the revenue coming into the government. The City of London was then able to use that revenue and invest in the sort of transportation infrastructure that it needed to solve these traffic concerns in the long term because demand for transportation services is only increasing, as more and more people move into the city. While London changed consumer behavior in the short term, it was able to raise money to solve the supply problem in the long term.

The simple truth about dynamic pricing that doesn't just have to be based on time. It can be based on location. It can be based on geography. It can be based on demand. Yes, it can be based on time but it can be interrelated with other various factors and that's where the efficacy really comes from.

Conditional-rules based dynamic pricing is best in markets where you have to compete with competitors or want to incentivize customers to act in certain ways. Moreover, conditional-rules based dynamic pricing can work in conjunction with your other pricing strategies. In fact, you should seek to actively combine conditional-rules with the rest of your pricing strategy to cover all possible outcomes that can unfold in the marketplace, these rules will kick in only as a response to other market participants' actions or they can be central to shaping those other market participants' actions. The latter was the case with London's congestion levy, the fact that the dynamic pricing scheme only activated within a certain radius, made people change their behavior proactively, lest they have to pay to be in the zone. Ultimately, it is this sort of flexibility that gives dynamic pricing an ontological advantage over fixed prices.

CHAPTER 11

PERSONALIZED PRICING

———

Imagine you are an extremely wealthy middle-aged business-person. As you drive your Lamborghini to the yacht club to meet up with some friends, you realize that you're running a few minutes late. This simply will not do. You put your foot on the accelerator, and the car takes off like a rocket ship. What is going through your head when you decide to endanger the public by speeding like this?

Let's indulge a counterfactual. Imagine you were an average American in your mid-20s. You're running late to a movie with friends, but you don't give in to your impulse to speed. Instead, you bite the bullet and show up fifteen minutes late. Why?

The intuitive answer is simply that a $350 speeding ticket means a lot more to the average American than it does to the wealthy driver. Both know that there is some chance that they can get away with speeding. But, the average American doesn't want to take the chance because the outcome where he gets caught is too financially devastating for him. To him, $350 is almost a full week's salary. Getting caught would mean less money for leisure like going to the movies, drinking with his friends, or going bowling. On the other hand, it the rich guy had to pay $350, it would tradeoff with exactly nothing meaningful in his life. For that reason, the fine doesn't even compute for the rich guy.

The question then is: should we index speeding tickets' financial penalties to income level? Should wealthier people have to pay more than average Americans? In other words, should we price discriminate against wealthy people? It seems that would be the only way to get them to internalize the costs of speeding. Moreover, it could generate more revenue for the state.

Would it be fair? Is the status quo fair, where the penalties are equivalent to average people taking a gut punch and rich people stubbing their toe momentarily? Ultimately, regardless of its merits, it is unlikely that the Government uses any sort of personalized pricing scheme in the near term, instead, the great movement toward personalized pricing in the status quo is coming from the private sector.

In personalized pricing schemes, every consumer is quoted a different price by the supplier based on the consumer's willingness to pay for a good. You may have a lot of questions about this specific strategy. How does personalized pricing even work? Don't most people agree on what something should cost anyway? Is this ethical? Of all the various forms of dynamic pricing, technologically powered personalized pricing is the one that raises the most eyebrows, and it is also the one with the potential to provoke the most backlash.

Personalized pricing in the private sector would look like Amazon charging you something different for the same good than it charges your neighbor who is scrolling through Amazon browsing the same good at the same time. In personalized pricing schemes, these decisions are solely based on who you are and their estimation of your own willingness to pay. While there may be ethical issues with personalized pricing done by businesses, there are also substantial strategic issues that simply make it a bad business practice in most cases broadly. There are some caveats to this general thesis, such as the fact that personalized pricing may be profitable for businesses with monopoly power. However, for either simple economic reasons or for reasons rooted in consumer backlash, trying to employ personalized pricing can be a kiss of death for a business that are looking to the practice in the near term.

Professor Michael Douma argues that it might not be economically sound to use personalized pricing. As a professor in the McDonough School of Business at Georgetown University, he has a very particular complaint. He doesn't like how Georgetown University charges its professors for parking. In the status quo, the more a professor makes, the more they are charged for parking. The most senior and tenured professors, therefore, are charged the most for spots in the underground garage. Adjunct professors and teaching assistants are charged the least for their designated spots. So far so good, right? At first, it seems that people who cannot afford higher prices get to pay lower prices.

Professor Douma then asked me to consider something that points out the flaw with that line of thinking: Imagine a world where everything is priced through discrimination. In other words, prices for each and every single good are more expensive for wealthier people and less expensive for poorer ones. He asked me, "What is the incentive for a wealthy person to work hard to make money anymore?"

In many ways, this same debate over personalized pricing was at the core of the Cold War ideological debate between Communism and Capitalism. If a wealthy person who makes a million dollars can afford the exact same bundle of goods that a poor person who makes a salary hovering around the poverty line can afford, why should the wealthy person continue to provide services that are demanded and rare if there are easier ways for him to have the same standard of living?

Growing up children constantly hear how the video game, or the toy in the aisle, or the even something as inexpensive as candy is too expensive to buy. Children are always upset to hear that. They wonder how can my parents be so mean? This is because kids don't really understand what expensive means. They don't internalize costs, so in a child's way of viewing the world- if my mom checks out the toy, I just get a new toy, without having to give anything up. Unfortunately, that's not how the world works. For each thing that you buy, you're trading the labor that you or a parent did to make the money that you are now spending. When a parent says the dreaded word "expensive", it is because they value the money that they earned more than you do, and they value the toy you want a lot less than you do.

As we grow up and work summer jobs or do chores, the concept of expensiveness becomes clearer and clearer. Yet a fundamental truth becomes clearer too: Valuations are subjective. I would pay any amount of money to be a soccer star for Manchester United, but my sister would pay less than nothing to be a soccer star as it holds no value for her. This pervasive truth about the economy first became clear to me on my sixth birthday.

On my car ride there, I knew exactly what I wanted. My favorite toys at the time were Legos. That day, I wanted not just any Lego set but one that could bolster my nascent Jedi collection of Lego Star Wars toys. My favorite Jedi was Anakin Skywalker (Boy, did it break my heart when he turned evil.). We finally arrived at Toys "R" Us and I ran into the store, going straight to the Lego aisle. I glanced around and I picked out a Lego set with some really cool characters. It had Obi-Wan! His lightsaber looked fantastic. So I picked it out, smugly proud of my decision.

On my car ride there, I knew exactly what I wanted. My favorite toys at the time were Legos. Today, I wanted not only any Lego set but one that could bolster my nascent Jedi collection of Lego Star Wars toys. My favorite Jedi was Anakin Skywalker (boy did it break my heart when he went evil). We finally arrived at Toys "R" Us and I ran into the store, going straight to the Lego aisle. I glanced around and I picked out a Lego set with some really cool characters. It had Obi-Wan! His lightsaber looked fantastic. So I picked it out, smugly proud of my decision.

My parents were far more skeptical. They kept asking me, "Are you sure?" Their tone did not inspire confidence. It struck me in a way that indicated that it was not too expensive (their usual objection) but rather not good enough. I didn't really understand why they were so surprised about my choice of

Lego set. I looked around again and I kept saying, "Yes, that's the one I want." Eventually, they agreed, and we went to check out. Yet as we checked out, the jarring memory of their skepticism came with us.

Many, many years later, I finally understood what had happened then. The Lego set I had chosen had only cost $5. Because it was my birthday, they were expecting me to choose something more expensive with bigger Lego sets or more characters or something. Not being children themselves, and certainly not interested in Jedi Lego toys, they were simply deriving value from the price tag. In their view, the more expensive something was, the better the present it would make. On the other hand, I was deriving value from the specific characters I wanted.

This story, in hindsight, illustrates a lot of salient points about pricing:

Firstly, each individual's valuation of a good is entirely subjective. Definitionally, it must be subjective, because no one can approximate what something is worth to me, more than I can. There are then at least two places where my valuation can diverge from your valuation. One is in approximating how much happiness I will get from any experience. The second is converting that approximation to a dollar amount. In the story earlier, I approximated the happiness I could get out of that small Lego set at a really high value because it would allow me to add a missing Jedi to my collection. My parents approximated it at some low value because they were using its list price as a way to approximate the quality of the set. Consequently, if I had to pay on my own for that set, I would be willing to pay well over $20. However, my parents- mistakenly thinking- they could make me happier with a different set, placed a dollar value on that set at simply its list price of $5 or even lower. Why people would pay only five dollars for something so cool now is something that really baffles me still. These subjective differences then create a big opportunity in the market.

This brings us to the second salient point. Price discrimination on the part of suppliers can exploit these subjective differences. There is an entire spectrum of buyers with kids like me on one end of the market and my parents on the other. But there is also a broader spectrum, of wealthier consumers and middle-class consumers, people more willing to spend money on toys and people less willing to do that. By discriminating prices between these types of people, suppliers like toy stores in some circumstances could make a lot of money.

For example, if Toys "R" Us had used a name-your-price tool similar to the way Priceline once had, then it would have found out that I valued the Lego set at far more than their internal valuation of $5. In doing so, they could have collected the entire $20 from me and made a far greater profit than they had before. This assumes some level of monopoly power whereby I can't go to another store and get it for cheaper, but generally, this is how price discrimination works, and when deployed well, it is incredibly powerful.

As Arik Levinson, an economics Professor at Georgetown University, explains, "Every business would like to know its demand curve so that it can price discriminate." In the past, there have been three things stopping them from doing that. First is the fear of intense backlash. Second is difficulty isolating a person's willingness to pay. Last is competition preventing anyone from gaining too much monopoly power.

In the modern world, only the first reason still remains in a lot of markets. Otherwise, through data analytics of the most mundane details such as which browser you use to access the Internet, companies can put together a profile of your willingness to pay for certain goods. Additionally, competition is notably absent from a lot of markets today because of competitive dynamics like network effects.

Personalized pricing is nothing new. Car salesman, who build a mental profile of how much you would be willing to pay, offer quotes for cars tailored specifically to the person who is trying to buy the car. Beyond car sales, a whole host of industries ranging from informal yard sales to e-commerce on sites like eBay employ some form of personalized pricing.

What is new in the market today is the scope of data and the methods that are being employed in developing personalized pricing schemes for online transactions. While talk of big data sounds very abstract, and a bit paranoid, companies like Facebook and Youtube today can build intensely precise profiles aggregating all sorts of personal information from all of the content you consume on their sites. They know where you live, which soccer team you support, how you spend your free time, and the broader themes tying small details of your life together.

That is the computing power, and level of detail, those types of big corporations are now able to achieve through the use of data analytics. In many cases, they might have an economic incentive to use that sort of information to price discriminate. Moreover, if companies gain the ability to do this nearly perfectly, without generating backlash, then this practice will proliferate to every corner of the market because the ability to profit from personalized pricing is unparalleled.

Anecdotal evidence of personalized pricing abounds. There are stories of people getting quotes at different prices on their phones and their laptops for the same items. Yet few companies will openly admit to doing personalized pricing online. However, ever the pioneer, Uber admitted to testing personalized pricing in certain cities in June 2017. In those areas, it not only used revenue management-based dynamic pricing but also actively tracked which neighborhoods people spent time in to build profiles of how much they would be willing to spend on transportation.

Moreover, the ethical dilemmas surrounding personalized pricing are not as clear-cut as they may initially seem. As Scott Kominers reported for Bloomberg at the time of Uber's admission, "While price discrimination can raise profits, it can also help society by enabling more people to access the market. We applaud college financial aid policies, for example, because they expand access to education – but they're a form of price discrimination, giving assistance to students who have less ability to pay, while charging full tuition to those with more resources." (Kominers).

However, Ariel Ezrachi, a professor of competition law at Oxford University takes the opposite view, he thinks that when compared to other forms of dynamic pricing, "personalized pricing is much more problematic. It's based on asymmetricity of information; it's only possible because the shopper doesn't know what information the seller has about them, and because the seller is able to create an environment where the shopper believes they are seeing the market price." (Walker).

One person, who would certainly feel betrayed by personalized pricing is Thomas Mulligan, a Professor of markets and ethics at Georgetown University. Professor Mulligan finds two underlying issues with personalized dynamic pricing in particular. Firstly, the idea of different prices for different people in any circumstance as inconsistent with his moral intuitions. According to him, economic justice comes from people being treated the same way for doing the same things. This sense of justice is a deep intuition embedded within each of us, a by-product of the axiom all men are created equal. He says, "when we see someone in the same spot that we are in getting a different reward, let's say, or in this case, paying a different price that does bother us, that does rankle our sense of moral justice." Secondly, Professor Mulligan contends that there is an economic case to be made against dynamic pricing. He starts with the premise that people evaluate how good their lives are comparative to others in similar situations. Consequently, he contends that if a person is quoted a higher price than someone else for the same good, then this eats away at his or her happiness. For example, if I buy a baseball ticket for $30 at the same time that you buy adjacent seats for $25, this makes me unhappier because you got a better deal than me, and this leaves me worse off. Therefore, dynamic pricing, where someone is left unhappier with their purchase, creates a form of market failure that needs to be corrected in his view.

So is personalized pricing inevitable in most markets going forward, absent Government regulation? The answer is not necessarily. It is important to note that market competition serves as a check on the practice of personalized pricing. This is because personalized pricing only works if the company doing it has market power. Otherwise, if you quote a rich guy a higher price, the rich guy will just go to the business that quotes him a lower price. You might say, but what if he doesn't have any options because everyone else is doing personalized pricing too. Well that means that there is space for some other company to join the market, and not do personalized pricing, and all those customers who can get cheaper prices elsewhere, will move to this new option. This is the reason why absent substantial monopoly power on the sale of a specific item, such that the rich guy has few options but to buy from you, personalized pricing is not economically sound.

Ethically, personalized pricing is still considered a gray area, or worse, in most people's minds. For that reason, personalized pricing may be a bridge too far in the status quo, as people might feel far more aggrieved by discrimination on the basis of personality as opposed to the time of consumption. While we've discussed "pricing contact theory", there is a substantial optical difference between personalized pricing and other forms of dynamic pricing because in other forms of dynamic pricing through savvy behavior, anyone can get a good deal, but in personalized pricing, that door is closed to you because of who you are. Equal treatment of people is a norm deeply embedded in our society and personalized pricing violates that norm more than other dynamic pricing practices do. Even if a business has monopoly power, to the extent that employing personalized pricing could be risking an entire brand, businesses would be wise to be risk-averse.

However, in the case, that personalized pricing is deployed on a mass scale, consumers will have to learn to shift their behavior to avoid being taken advantage of. By reverse engineering exactly how consumer profiles are built, consumers might be able to exploit weaknesses. For example, if Uber bases its personalized prices off of the neighborhoods you stay in, then one solution would be to turn off location services unless you are in a bad neighborhood, to throw off Uber's sense of where you spend your time.

Overall, the best check on preventing abusive use of personalized pricing is going to be competition in the marketplace, because of any abusive personalized prices from one firm, open up opportunities for other firms to steal consumers. As long as Lyft maintains robust competition, Uber cannot afford to quote personalized prices, lest consumers start cross-checking prices with Lyft. In this way, competition will create equilibriums that protect consumers. However, the absence of competition could move us down a darker road.

While personalized pricing might be justified for a Government to do as a form of punishment, as in the case of speeding tickets, or in the case of college tuition as a way to extend access to the market to more people, it is unwise for businesses, especially ones without substantial market power, to move towards personalized pricing as a general pricing strategy. To do so is to provoke public backlash, new competitors, and possibly even government oversight or regulation. At this stage in the game, when it comes to personalized pricing an aversion dashed with a hint of curiosity at other business' market practices is the best path forward.

PART 3

CONSUMING SMARTER

CHAPTER 12

HOW DO CONSUMERS BENEFIT?

————

According to the United States Social Security Administration, my expected total lifespan is 82.4 years. That's when the Government anticipates I will die. How optimistic of them...

For the sake of this argument, let's assume you live for 100 years. Converted into hours, that's only 876,000 hours. You'll spend a fourth of that sleeping. So in the best case, your waking time on this planet is roughly 660,000 hours. That's it.

We don't know what happens when those 660,000 waking hours are all spent. Maybe we lose consciousness like before we were born. Maybe there are supernatural forces that take us to heaven or hell. Maybe we get reincarnated. Regardless,

660,000 waking hours on this planet are all we know for certain that we have.

Yet if you talk to the average person or even the average economist, everyone is always talking about how much money they need to budget. Why do we think that way? If we could live forever, then we could afford anything we wanted to because we would have an infinite amount of time to produce the resources necessary to do that. But we can't live forever—this is where the need to budget really comes from. Yet too often, we discount how valuable our time is and overweight how valuable our money is.

We only have 660,000 waking hours. Do you really want to spend one of those in line? Or would you rather let prices float, pay a few more dollars, and save that hour and spend it enjoying your life with your friends?

Imagine you're just standing in line waiting at the DMV. Imagine the line snakes outside around the mall. You have to wait in this line for four hours. You slowly inch toward the desk, and eventually, you get there. Reflect on that experience. You had been wasting your time before you got to that desk. Think about the frustration you feel in that moment. Don't you regret the fraction of your scarce minutes on this planet you spent in that line?

Yes, sometimes dynamic pricing might raise the price of scarce goods. But often, it will also decrease times you have to wait to acquire those goods. For example, the time you spend waiting for an Uber decreases because of surge pricing. The time you spend waiting for your reservation at a restaurant can decrease if the restaurant uses dynamic pricing. As dynamic pricing proliferates in more and more markets, these minutes and hours add up.

As Henry David Thoreau famously said, "The price of anything is the amount of life you exchange for it." When you're on your deathbed, you will not regret the additional few dollars you had to pay per transaction. You probably would do anything for another hour on this planet, though. Framed in this way, there is a broader benefit dynamic pricing offers to consumers that hasn't been properly internalized in a lot of instances.

The added time is certainly the most dramatic countervailing benefit, but there are other tangible benefits too. Seyhan, the owner of a restaurant in D.C. called Georgetown Gourmet, explained how he tries to increase prices as little as possible. His adjustment mechanism is to control the quantity as much as possible before he has to revise prices upwards as lightly as possible. As he explains, when "the cost of the inventory goes up, for example, for the avocado I used to charge a $1, now I charge a $1.50, and the reason is that the avocado tripled in price." Now imagine if quality and quantity were held constant but prices were allowed to freely float in that market. People would lose by having to pay more, but they would gain by actually getting the quantity of avocado they would like in their food.

While we should recognize that prices are often lower than normal because of dynamic pricing, even when prices increase, we as consumers must weigh how important countervailing benefits are compared to meager financial costs. But what if you have done all that, and still the higher price in unpalatable as a tradeoff for the main countervailing benefits of time and quality? Are there ways to traverse the new pricing landscape to get the maximum benefit? If you follow this very simple three-step process, there most certainly are: First, identify your goal. Second, understand your means. Third, adapt your behavior.

STEP ONE: IDENTIFY YOUR GOAL

At different times in your life, given the external circumstances, you may be looking to make different purchases. Moreover, your goals may differ from purchase to purchase. For example, I may be looking to save a lot of money when it comes to big-ticket items, and I may be looking for the most convenience when it comes to small-ticket items. The fact that prices are always changing can actually be a tremendous boost to consumers because it allows you to isolate those times in the market where you can get exactly what you want. However, to first get there you must decide what the goal of your purchase is. For example, if you are buying food, is the goal of your purchase to get food as soon as possible or as cheaply as possible? While there may be ways to achieve both objectives, you must first decide what matters most to you.

STEP TWO: UNDERSTAND THE MEANS

Recognize that dynamic pricing is not arbitrary, though it might seem so at times. Every business that utilizes dynamic pricing does so with some type of logic encoded into either a set of rules or an algorithm.

If the format of dynamic pricing the business uses is fixed or conditional rules-based, you can use their blueprint as a guide to achieve your goals very easily. For example, almost every restaurant has their happy hours listed on their website. If you know in advance that you want to eat at a certain place, you can go during the hours the happy hour menu tells you will be the cheapest if saving money is your goal. Rather simple, right?

But what if the company uses something like revenue management dynamic pricing or personalized pricing and their pricing system is seemingly opaque? Do not despair—instead, understand two things. One, most businesses do not do revenue management in-house, instead relying on another provider to do it for them. Because this is true, you only need to research the one provider (i.e. Uber) to understand everyone within the service (i.e. all Uber drivers). Two, if you want something, chances are someone else does too. Because of this, there is probably a whole host of literature already out there on any given dynamic pricing provider. Due to these two reasons, you can often reverse-engineer the broad strokes of the algorithm that any given business uses in order to use that as a blueprint to achieve your goal.

In the common caricature, the epitome of optimization and complicated algorithms is Uber, which means if you can reverse-engineer Uber's algorithm with careful precision, then anyone else is fair game too. In fact, other people have already done this. A study conducted by Le Chen, Alan Mislove and Christo Wilson from Northeastern University revealed many of the secrets behind Uber's surge pricing algorithm. Studying the market of Manhattan, they uncovered a few key findings. Primarily they concluded that "86% of the time there is no surge in Manhattan." (Chen, Mislove, and Wilson). Moreover, they also found that in NYC the majority of surges were within a x1.5 multiplier. What does this mean for consumers? (Chen, Mislove, and Wilson).

Well, it means that if you're in NYC and trying to get the best deal possible, you won't have to worry about surging most of the time. Moreover, even when you do, it will be within a limited range that while slightly more expensive is not exorbitantly so. But what if you're in a diffcrent Uber market where the reality isn't so appealing, or what if you're in NYC and this still isn't good enough for you? What if you want a guaranteed lack of surge pricing? Well, the same researchers also found that in many of their sample,s the majority of surges did not last more than five minutes. They also found that Uber breaks cities down into grids, so if you're in an adjacent grid, you will no longer be charged surge.

This type of critical information is available on the Internet for almost every type of dynamic pricing provider. For example, there are many articles about how to get the best prices on Amazon, when prices are constantly changing. Simple research can easily help you achieve your goal. However, if you want to understand how pricing works on an even more precise level, you can do things like join the markelplace as a provider. In the case of Uber or Lyft, you can "join" as a driver to see what the interface is like and how it works. Moreover, you can check the driver app on a day-to-day basis to see where surge pricing is happening and then avoid those places. No matter how opaque the system, the means to understand it exists out there, and it is your job as a consumer to find that information.

STEP 3: ADAPT YOUR BEHAVIOR

Once you understand how something like surge pricing works, what do you do from there? How does knowing that surge often only lasts five minutes help a consumer like you? For one, it gives you the information you need to achieve your goals. Extending this example, if by waiting another few minutes you can get your Uber at a much cheaper price, then you ought to wait, especially if saving money is your priority. This same goal can be achieved by walking a few blocks over to get out of a surge grid and into a non-surging grid.

Adapting your behavior doesn't just mean working within the parameters of Uber or Lyft or any other marketplace that dynamically prices, but rather to go beyond them or play them against each other. For example, many apps exist that can give you quotes from Uber, Lyft and other less-well-known ride-sharing services given your location and destination. You can then choose between those options. While all of these platforms are probably dynamically pricing and responding to the same phenomenon—for example, they might all be surging—often their algorithms work in very different ways, which means that one may be surging a lot more than another service. By making using these consumer tools a habit, you can benefit substantially at no cost to you.

CONCLUSION

HOW YOUR BUSINESS CAN PROSPER FROM DYNAMIC PRICING

What does it tell you when Sears, Kohl's and the Home Depot are all using electronic price displays so that they can begin to dynamically price in person at their stores? It tells us that we are witnessing something truly special—the extinction of the price tag in a whole host of industries, including retail.

Yet still, some people ask, "Why does dynamic pricing really matter?" Does it really make a difference if a sandwich costs a dollar less or a car ride costs three dollars more? An unfortunate sentiment is shared by too many people: Too many think dynamic pricing belongs in the periphery of economics. This is wrong.

Uber on its own is worth over $50 billion. Each transaction individually might seem like it is not a big deal. But taken together, dynamic pricing has—and will increasingly have— an absolutely massive impact on the economy if you simply aggregate the scope and magnitude of dynamic transactions. When you then consider how deeply each economic transaction cascades throughout the economic framework of the country, it becomes abundantly clear that this is one of the most pressing economic changes in the modern economy. This is especially true given the linkages inherent in the economic marketplace, but ever more powerful because of globalization and technological advancement. A favorite story of mine is one that Nobel Laureate George Akerlof relayed to me explaining how those linkages work:

One of Professor Akerlof's first insights into economics was based on these linkages. When he was really young, his father lost his job. This was really hard for him and his family and set about an amount of reckoning for the young George. Thinking generally about the issue of unemployment, Professor Akerlof intuited that if his father lost his job, then his father would stop spending money. The money that his father spends is someone else's income. In turn, someone else would lose their job, creating a chain reaction until everyone lost their jobs.

This simplistic model, though very sophisticated for a child, is insufficient to further a broad understanding of economics. However, it illustrates an important point—we're all in this together. If dynamic pricing is an economic evolution that has a profound impact on our relationships, then we as a society ought to take a deeper look into its consequences and benefits.

Professor Akerlof told me that when he was younger, one of his teachers asked him what he wanted for Christmas. She expected him to say a firetruck or action figures. George Akerlof, having grown up in Pittsburgh, told his teacher he wanted a factory. He concluded that if he had a factory, he could afford any of the other things he might have asked Santa for.

This again clarifies economics with its simplicity. If we had an infinite amount of money, prices would not exist. But we don't have an infinite amount of money. Each society needs to determine how to ration limited resources among its people to lead to the most socially acceptable outcome. Prices are how we ration those goods. Those arbitrary numbers tell us how much of one thing we should be willing to give up for another thing. This leads to a process of trading until each of us gets what gives us the most benefits given our income and time constraints. In "economics speak," prices serve to quantify opportunity costs. Using dynamic pricing, we are able to do that in the most efficient manner possible.

There are many forms and types of dynamic pricing that have gained traction in the market. Moreover, the rise of new technological tools and development of online marketplaces has made dynamic pricing increasingly necessary. However, while consumer backlash risk may be holding the market back in the short term, because of "pricing contact theory," it will not in the longer term. Now is the chance to adapt to the market before your competitors do to get ahead and stay ahead. If one thing is clear, dynamic pricing is only just getting started.

Understanding this key insight from this book, your most important takeaway is that adapting to dynamic pricing is an inevitability for your business. If you understand that, you understand that now is when you can get a jump on your competitors. Now is when you can use dynamic pricing to turbo-charge your business. You should approach this general concept with a fierce urgency because it really could be the difference-maker not only in terms of padding profits but also in terms of your very survival. Retail both across the country and internationally has been collapsing. Restaurants specifically have suffered from a supply glut over the last few years, with many now closing their doors because of intensive competition. Operating in that enviornment is not easy, and any tool that can help you become successful needs to be implemented. So, how can you use dynamic pricing to save your business? Actually, it's simple if you follow the five following steps:

STEP 1: CALIBRATE YOUR
STRATEGY TO YOUR MARKET

Figure out what kind of market you are in and who you are competing against. If you have an intense battle against a rival like Wingo's did, maybe conditional-rules based pricing rooted in competitor prices is the best option for you. Otherwise, if you are simply suffering from a surplus of perishable goods, maybe revenue management is best for you. If you have significant market power, perhaps personalized pricing is the most revenue-maximizing option for you. Each previous chapter devoted to specific types of dynamic pricing delineates which types of markets most favor which types of dynamic pricing. Whatever the case may be, understand your market and calibrate your strategy accordingly.

Once you have chosen one or a combination of the types of dynamic pricing on show in this book, it is time for the next step.

STEP 2: FIND THE BEST TOOL FOR
YOUR CHOSEN STRATEGY

Unless you are a very large corporation with substantial computational and logistical resources, you are going to want to get outside help when it comes to dynamic pricing. For example, restaurants that struggle with shifting demand throughout the day and significant stagnant periods can get access to state-of-the-art revenue-management tools by partnering with Dynos, where they can use our revenue-management tools while having a marketplace platform to reach consumers. An interaction Seyhan Duru and I had right before the Dynos launch illustrates this point.

Seyhan is the owner of Georgetown Gourmet, a fantastic panini and sandwich shop in D.C. One of the first times we met, I pitched him on the idea of partnering with Dynos, while Dynos was still going through development. He said, "Yes, let's do it." He expected us to be done in a few weeks. Almost four months later, the app was just getting finished and ready to go live. After that, it took us another few weeks to do all the testing required. After all of this was done, we finished all the grunt work logistics set-up. In fact, when I went in to set up the tablet for his business to receive Dynos orders, once we finally neared launch, he said, "And now we're another step closer to the moon."

The point is, we were devoted to developing this platform full-time and it still took us forever to finish off even the most basic functionalities. Now imagine trying to develop it on your own for your business to use on the side. It is simply not feasible. Moreover, it won't be as effective unless all the restaurants are listed in one place, where consumers can easily see everything in one location, as local Georgetown students and residents are able to on the Dynos app.

Depending on your business, there may be many tools that are right for you—you might want a marketplace like Dynos or simply a computation tool that can generate the right numbers. Look to what your competitors are doing and using, if you have any. Otherwise, just a simple search, "[my industry] dynamic pricing solutions," will return all sorts of tools that you can compare. For example, for retailers, there are companies like Perfect Price and Revenue Analytics that show up when you Google search "retail dynamic pricing solutions." Moreover, there are more startups in this space every day increasing the depth of your options.

STEP 3: DO A TRIAL RUN

Once you have the tool you want, do a trial run with certain segments of your menu or product line, either on specific days or in specific locations. Keep this limited. Most importantly, gauge the consumer response to how you are pricing. Connect with your customers in person and on social media. Listen to what they have to say. Most importantly, explain what you are trying to do. Especially if you are a small business, you will be shocked by how understanding customers can be if you engage with them in an honest way.

While you are doing the trial run, work out any logistical kinks. Moreover, figure out if dynamic pricing has been economically beneficial in the natural experiment that you are running. If it has, how much so? How can this be improved? Is it reasonable to expect the same results if you move to dynamic pricing more often? Have answers to all of these questions before you move forward.

STEP 4: WEIGH COSTS AND BENEFITS

The costs are compliance and logistics and the larger risk of consumer backlash. The benefits are potentially double-digit percentage increases in revenue and profits for businesses in the right industries using the right dynamic pricing tools. Weigh these things against each other. Do you honestly expect backlash? How widespread? Are there ways to mitigate it? How much do you expect dynamic pricing to help your business? Ask your dynamic pricing tool for numbers and case studies on other businesses in similar fields like yours. Ask for their projections. Look to the results of your trial run. If everything went well and consumer backlash is not as much of an issue, then it is time to move forward.

STEP 5: ANNOUNCE YOUR NEW PRICING POLICY.

This is the last place to escape in case backlash does materialize. In the interim between announcing your policy and implementing it, you can reverse. However, if you have made it this far and some small amounts of backlash materialize, I would recommend riding out that small amount, because not everyone will always be happy with price changes, and some backlash is to be expected.

Most importantly, this is a phase where you can engage with consumers on a broad scale and explain why the changes are necessary. It helps to be a small business, but even if you are a larger business, find different ways to frame the policy change. Never use the words "surge pricing" or even "dynamic pricing." Instead, try terms like "discount pricing," terms that emphasize the benefits to consumers instead of the costs. Ultimately, those that are able to best connect with consumers are going to be the ones that are best able to explain not only the logic behind it all but also the story for why it is necessary. Tell the stories of the positive aspects of your trial run on social media and in any advertising. By getting those stories out there, you may even see a spike in the total number of people in the store as consumers respond to the buzz around the policy changes.

Overall, while not guaranteed, by following these five steps, you can maximize your chances of being successful at dynamic pricing. In turn, dynamic pricing will maximize the welfare of your business and the economy generally. Don't wait until your competitors have already implemented dynamic pricing to do it for your own business. Instead, be the reason your competitors are having to implement dynamic pricing.

BIBLIOGRAPHY

Allport, Gordon W. "The Nature of Prejudice." (1954) Web.

Beckett, Andy. "The Truth about London's Congestion Charge."
The Guardian, Guardian News and Media, 10 Feb. 2003,
www.theguardian.com/politics/2003/feb/10/london.
congestioncharging.

Chen, Le, Alan Mislove, and Christo Wilson. "Peeking Beneath
the Hood of Uber". Proceedings of the 2015 Internet
Measurement Conference. Web.

"Disney Discovers Peak Pricing." *The Economist*, The Economist
Newspaper, 29 Feb. 2016, www.economist.com/blogs/
freeexchange/2016/02/price-discrimination-land.

Goldstein, Jacob, et al. "Episode 633: The Birth And Death Of The
Price Tag." *NPR*, NPR, 17 June 2015, www.npr.org/templates/
transcript/transcript.php?storyId=415287577.

Goldstein, Jacob, et al. "Episode 633: The Birth And Death Of The

Price Tag." *NPR*, NPR, 17 June 2015, www.npr.org/templates/
transcript/transcript.php?storyId=415287577.

Hays, Constance L. "Variable-Price Coke Machine Being Tested."
The New York Times, The New York Times, 27 Oct. 1999,
www.nytimes.com/1999/10/28/business/variable-price-coke-
machine-being-tested.html.

Irby, Kate. "Why New York City's Drunk Driving Accidents Have
Gone Way down since 2011." *Miamiherald*, Miami Herald,
6 Apr. 2017, www.miamiherald.com/news/nation-world/
national/article143043959.html.

Isaac, Mike. "Uber's C.E.O. Plays With Fire." *The New York
Times*, The New York Times, 23 Apr. 2017, www.nytimes.
com/2017/04/23/technology/travis-kalanick-pushes-uber-
and-himself-to-the-precipice.html?mtrref=www.google.
com&gwh=CDA954B83292965002D01D145139900B&gwt=
pay.

Kominers, Scott Duke. "Uber's New Pricing Idea Is Good
Theory, Risky Business." *Bloomberg.com*, Bloomberg, 13
June 2017, www.bloomberg.com/view/articles/2017-06-13/
uber-s-new-pricing-idea-is-good-theory-risky-business.

Leonhardt, David. "Why Variable Pricing Fails at the Vending
Machine." *The New York Times*, The New York Times, 27 June
2005, www.nytimes.com/2005/06/27/business/why-variable-
pricing-fails-at-the-vending-machine.html?mtrref=www.
google.com&gwh=C18D245DA5BA887460A06F8D15B-
31B7A&gwt=pay.

Lowrey, Annie. "Is Uber's Surge-Pricing an Example of High-Tech

Gouging?" *The New York Times*, The New York Times, 10 Jan.
2014, www.nytimes.com/2014/01/12/magazine/is-ubers-surge-
pricing-an-example-of-high-tech-gouging.html.

"Mad Men." Bianchi, Ed, director. Season 1, episode 3.

Morris, Nigel. "The Big Question: Has the Congestion Charge
Been Effective in Reducing London's Traffic?" *The
Independent*, Independent Digital News and Media, 12
Feb. 2008, www.independent.co.uk/news/uk/home-news/
the-big-question-has-the-congestion-charge-been-effective-
in-reducing-londons-traffic-781505.html.

Nolan, Christopher, director. *The Dark Knight*. Warner Brothers,
2009.

Overby, Stephanie. "For San Francisco Giants, Dynamic Pricing
Software Hits a Home Run." *CIO*, CIO, 29 June 2011, www.cio.
com/article/2406673/business-intelligence/for-san-francisco-
giants--dynamic-pricing-software-hits-a-home-run.html.

Patton, Leslie. "McDonald's to Cut Prices on Drinks as Industry
Slumps." *Bloomberg*, 22 Feb. 2017, www.bloomberg.com/
news/articles/2017-02-22/mcdonald-s-to-cut-prices-on-
drinks-as-fast-food-industry-slumps+.

"Pricing the Surge." *The Economist*, The Economist
Newspaper, 29 Mar. 2014, www.economist.com/news/
finance-and-economics/21599766-microeconomics-ubers-at-
tempt-revolutionise-taxi-markets-pricing-surge.

Sachdev, Ameet. "Baseball Teams Get Dynamic with Ticket
Pricing." *Chicago Tribune*, Chicago Tribune, 12 May
2013, articles.chicagotribune.com/2013-05-12/business/

ct-biz-0512-stub-hub--20130512_1_stubhub-bleacher-tick-et-ticket-reselling.

Sahay, Arvind. "How to Reap Higher Profits With Dynamic Pricing." *MIT Sloan Management Review*, 1 July 1007, sloanreview.mit.edu/article/how-to-reap-higher-profits-with-dynamic-pricing/.

Thompson, Derek. "The History of Sears Predicts Nearly Everything Amazon Is Doing." *The Atlantic*, Atlantic Media Company, 25 Sept. 2017, www.theatlantic.com/business/archive/2017/09/sears-predicts-amazon/540888/.

Walker, Tim. "How Much…? The Rise of Dynamic and Personalised Pricing." *The Guardian*, Guardian News and Media, 20 Nov. 2017, www.theguardian.com/global/2017/nov/20/dynamic-personalised-pricing.

Wolf, Cam. "Paul Newman's Rolex Daytona Just Sold for $17.8 Million." *GQ*, GQ, 27 Oct. 2017, www.gq.com/story/paul-newman-rolex-daytona-auction.